The Man Who Bought Alaska
A short biography of William H. Seward

Celebrating Alaska's Sesquicentennial–
150 years as part of the U.S. (1867 - 2017)

By Michael Dunham

Library of Congress Control Number: 2016961653

ISBN: 978-1-57833-660-9

First Printing: January, 2017

Editor: Flip Todd, 𝕿𝖔𝖉𝖉 𝕮𝖔𝖒𝖒𝖚𝖓𝖎𝖈𝖆𝖙𝖎𝖔𝖓𝖘
Book Design: Vered R. Mares, 𝕿𝖔𝖉𝖉 𝕮𝖔𝖒𝖒𝖚𝖓𝖎𝖈𝖆𝖙𝖎𝖔𝖓𝖘

Printed in the United States
through Alaska Print Brokers, Anchorage, Alaska

Published by:
𝕿𝖔𝖉𝖉 𝕮𝖔𝖒𝖒𝖚𝖓𝖎𝖈𝖆𝖙𝖎𝖔𝖓𝖘
611 E. 12th Ave.
Anchorage, Alaska 99501-4603
(907) 274-TODD (8633)
Fax: (907) 929-5550
sales@toddcom.com • WWW.ALASKABOOKSANDCALENDARS.COM
with other offices in Juneau and Fairbanks, Alaska

Acknowledgments

The author wishes to thank the staffs of the University of Rochester River Campus Rush Rhees Library, the Seward House Museum in Auburn, New York and the Jilkaat Kwaan Heritage Center in Klukwan, Alaska for access to original documents and items pertaining to the transfer of Alaska from Russia to the United States. In addition to the sources listed in the bibliography, important information and insights were shared in personal communications with Herbert Hope, Grand President of the Alaska Native Brotherhood, prior to his death in 1999. A career official with the Bureau of Indian Affairs, he was an assiduous historian who collected oral histories from members of his family, Tlingits of Sitka, whose memories reached back to the Russian era.

This book is part of a two book set:

The Man Who Bought Alaska
William H. Seward

&

The Man Who Sold Alaska
Tsar Alexander II of Russia

Contents

The Man Who Bought Alaska

A short biography of William H. Seward

By Michael Dunham

One: A Good Hand

The game of whist requires the player to analyze several factors at once and act quickly when he sees an advantage. Similar to bridge, whist was the rage among educated classes in the 1800s. William Henry Seward, the 24th Secretary of State of the United States of America, was good at it.

Late on the evening of Friday, March 29, 1867, Seward and his family were at the card table in the parlor of his home near the White House. A servant entered to announce the arrival of Edouard de Stoeckl, the Russian minister to America. The ambassador was shown in as Seward continued with the game.

Seward's son Frederick wrote down the conversation.

Said Stoeckl, "I have a dispatch from my Government by cable. The Emperor gives his consent to the cession."

He was talking about the proposed sale of Russian America to the United States. The subject had been discussed quietly between the two governments for decades before the American Civil War. Since the end of the war negotiations had become serious. In the previous two months Seward and Stoeckl had spent many hours working out the details.

The region now known as Alaska contained vast resources, but Seward saw it mainly in terms of geopolitics. The coast and islands of the territory connected the New World with Asia. And, Seward felt certain, his country's future would gravitate toward the Pacific. Such was America's destiny and Alaska was crucial to making it happen.

"Tomorrow, if you like, I will come to the department and we can enter upon the treaty," Stoeckl continued.

Smiling, Seward put down his cards and pushed away the whist table. "Why wait till tomorrow, Mr. Stoeckl?" he said. "Let us make the treaty tonight."

"But your department is closed," Stoeckl protested. "You have no clerks and your secretaries are scattered about the town."

"Never mind that," Seward responded, rising from his chair. "If you can muster your legation together before midnight, you will find me awaiting you at the department, which will be open and ready for business."

"In less than two hours," Frederick recalled, "light was streaming out of the windows at the Department of State." Stoeckl, Seward and their staffs put the final touches on the treaty that would sell 663,000 square miles to the United States for the equivalent of two cents an acre. In terms of area, it remains the largest single addition to the country after the Louisiana Purchase.

If modern Americans can name one person who served as Secretary of State before they were born, that person is probably William Henry Seward. If they can name one thing Seward did, they most likely know him as the man who bought Alaska.

But it was by no means the only important act of his tenure or of his life.

William Seward was an early and earnest advocate of civil rights. His robust defense of the disadvantaged probably cost him his chance at winning the highest office in the land. He was a far-sighted diplomat whose ideas and actions continue to shape foreign policy. He was an adroit negotiator whose success in keeping Europe out of the Civil War was as critical to the North's victory as the battles of Ulysses S. Grant and the policies of Abraham Lincoln.

One can reasonably say that, had Seward not lived, the United States of America, if it still existed at all, would not be the country it is today.

Two: Young Man in a Young Land

The fledgling nation had just survived its first great test when William Seward was born on May 16, 1801.

The United States was only 12 years old. European powers expected that the experiment in government would be temporary. They were sure that, without a monarch, the individual states would soon break into impoverished, ineffectual entities begging Britain to protect them against the Indians, foreign invasion and each other.

For the first eight years, George Washington, the military hero who led the colonists to victory, maintained order as President. There was little dissent when Washington passed the office to his Vice President, John Adams, in 1796. But in 1800 a bitterly contested campaign for the presidency erupted between Adams and Thomas Jefferson. Jefferson won.

Would Adams allow his opponent to take his place? Or would he follow the course taken by rulers throughout history and use the army to stay in power? Some thought the hour of dissolution had come.

To the amazement of these skeptics — and of posterity — that did not happen. Power peacefully transferred from one elected head of state to another. Adams quietly departed the capital and went home. He certainly felt cheated, unfairly deposed by lesser men, out-maneuvered by a canny foe. And, if he chose to fight, the small federal army at his disposal might have kept half of the territory under his control.

But that would have made him no different than the autocrats he had worked so hard to defeat militarily and intellectually. John Adams truly believed in the idea of a government of laws, not of men, and sincerely felt that a leader granted authority through the consent of his fellow citizens was morally bound to relinquish that authority when those citizens requested it.

That was the attitude of Washington, Jefferson and a significant portion of the citizenry who had any say in the elections, which is to say white men with some property.

Such a man was Samuel Swezy Seward of Florida, New York. He was an important figure in the hamlet of a dozen buildings — doctor, farmer, merchant and judge. He and his wife Mary Jennings had six children. William was the fourth.

In later years William Seward would recount tales of witches that permeated his youth. There were witches in the kitchen and above the school building. He slipped into the one-room school with the older children when he was barely five. Suddenly the sky was darkened by an eclipse and he thought that the witches would emerge "and make short work of us all. Crying vociferously, (I) ran for my life homeward."

North America in 1806 was filled with terrors known and unknown, inhabited by small bands of people surrounded by wilderness. The population was just over five million, nearly a million of whom were slaves.

Some of those slaves belonged to Samuel Seward. "I found their apartment more attractive than the parlor," William recalled. "They were vivacious and loquacious, as well as affectionate toward me." He taught the slave children to read and Samuel allowed them to attend school with his son.

Most Americans lived near the ports of the eastern seaboard. Florida, 50 miles from New York City, was somewhat in the hinterlands. To the west lay untold miles of forests and prairies, deserts and mountains that no citizen of the United States had ever seen.

Mighty Spain dominated the Caribbean Sea, Mexico and most of South America. On the Pacific side of North America, 2,500 miles from New York, they established a series of missions as far north as San Francisco.

Britain claimed the territory from the Great Lakes to the North Pole. But aside from towns on the St. Lawrence River and along the North Atlantic there were few settlers in the region.

Russia was the third European empire with substantial claims in the New World, a handful of fortified trading posts, mostly on islands in the far North Pacific.

It's doubtful that any maps young Seward might have seen included the Spanish or Russian settlements in North America. The northern edge of the continent and the expanse between the Atlantic and Pacific oceans was shown empty.

Yet it was not vacant. An estimated 600,000 Native Americans lived between the two oceans. The white settlers of New York disdained and feared them. Memories of raids and wars still ran strong. Seward often heard how his grandfather had survived the "Indian massacre" at the battle of Minisink, when militiamen were routed by British and Iroquois forces in the Revolutionary War. Ammunition ran out and the fight finished with merciless hand-to-hand combat at which the Indians excelled.

Seward may not have been told how the Continental Army retaliated by destroying scores of Iroquois towns and villages in northwestern New York.

The American Revolution was a defeat for the British, but a disaster for Eastern Indians who sided with the Crown. For 25 years after the War of Independence skirmishes continued. Such uprisings were relentlessly suppressed. The tribes crowded onto reservations or departed to the West.

Suppression was also the fate of Indians who lived close to the Spanish missions in California. Whole villages were captured and forced to do unpaid labor. Those who escaped or tried to fight back were hunted down and killed.

Sometimes, however, the Indians won. The year after Seward was born, Tlingit Indians in Southeast Alaska mounted a coordinated attack that wiped out Russian garrisons in Yakutat and Sitka. It took two years of planning and the propitious arrival of a warship for the Russian-American Company agent Alexander Baranov to retake Sitka. Under siege, deserted by his English allies, out of ammunition and perhaps beset by an epidemic, the Tlingit leader Katlian (K'alyaan) managed a strategic retreat.

Baranov rebuilt his post and named it New Archangel. It would become the power base from which he cut a deal with Katlian. The Tlingits supplied the Russians with furs and the Russians supplied the Tlingits with goods from China and the rapidly mechanizing Western world. New Archangel flourished with mutual prosperity and Baranov set his sights on a new prize: California.

All of this happened thousands of miles from New York. But Russian America became a lot closer in 1803 when, for $15 million, President Jefferson acquired 828,000 square miles of French claims on the west side of the Mississippi River. The Louisiana Purchase effectively doubled the size of the United States.

Out of the northwest part of the purchase the Columbia River flowed through a region loosely claimed by Britain and Spain, though neither had any settlements there. Jefferson was quick to stake it for America. He encouraged fur trader John Jacob Astor to build a Pacific post, Astoria. The station could only be reached by a 16,000 mile voyage around the tip of South America, a trip that took months.

And yet the ships came. Like Astor and Jefferson himself, the men who sailed those ships shared a supreme optimism about the future and an unsinkable conviction in the social and personal benefits of commerce and liberty, along with a contempt for monarchy. To one degree or another, most Americans felt the same way.

This belief permeated learned discussions in Boston, Philadelphia and New York. It also ran strong among the common folk of farming villages like Florida, New York. Seward saw a school performance of Joseph Addison's play "Cato," about the stoic Roman who stood up to Caesar. "It made me a hater of military and imperial usurpation for life," he wrote.

The annual celebrations of Independence Day thrilled him with their pageantry and declarations, military music and parades. "My first conception of the dignity and destiny of our country arose out of these rural festivities," he wrote. "I suppose I shall die loyal to New York and to the Federal Union."

His patriotism intensified with the War of 1812. He glowed with pride at reports — false, as it turned out — that American troops had conquered Canada. He seethed at the news that British troops had burned Washington, D.C. He wept on hearing of the defeat of Napoleon, "Because I had come to regard him as an ally of the United States."

Andrew Jackson's stunning victory in the Battle of New Orleans, though unimportant strategically, gave a huge boost to national morale.

But for the Native Americans living east of the Mississippi, the War of 1812 was a calamity on par with their loss in the American Revolution. The Shawnee leader Tecumseh convinced a coalition of tribes to join with the British in pushing back settlers encroaching on Indian lands. He died at the Battle of the Thames in Ontario, Canada in 1813. With him died the possibility of an independent American Indian nation occupying any significant amount of land.

Conflicts between the U.S Army and Indian tribes east of the Mississippi continued for another generation, but indigenous people won none of them.

While the British and Americans fought with each other, the Russians gained ground. They built Fort Ross north of San Francisco and a station on the Farallon Islands outside the Golden Gate. From these posts they harvested seal and sea otter under the very noses of the Spanish.

Almost unnoticed in the commotion was Astoria. Early in the war English officials arrived from Canada and ordered the Americans to leave.

The United States' little piece of the Pacific was gone.

Three: The Prodigal Son

In 1810 news traveled at the speed of a horse. For those without horses, a five mile trip could be a major undertaking that occupied a good part of the day.

That meant that when William Seward, at age nine, outgrew the little school in Florida, he had to board with relatives in Goshen, six miles by road, in order to attend a larger academy.

His account of his younger years hints that he was the target of bullies, which might explain why he tended to side with underdogs as an adult. To the bigger boys of Goshen, he was a hick from a tiny village, impetuous, with unruly red hair and ears that stuck out from his head like oars. And he was small; he never grew taller than five feet, six inches. He was the runt even of his own family.

His size and precarious health were among the reasons why Samuel Seward decided that, of all his sons, this one would receive a college education. Physical labor, he feared, would be too hard for the boy.

After a year William returned to Florida where a new school had been built. He studied a broad curriculum from 5 o'clock in the morning until 9 P.M. Somehow, he also found time to listen to the political debates that transpired daily in his father's store. "Men were more intensely earnest than they are now," he recalled.

Those lively country store forums shaped his intellect more than all of the Latin he was forced to memorize.

In 1816 he left "the sweet little valley in which I was cradled" to attend Union College in Schenectady. For the first time in his life he saw a steamboat. Fifty years later he still felt the thrill. "What a magnificent palace! What a prodigy of power!" he wrote.

The boat took him to Albany, the biggest city he had ever seen. In later years he recalled that the first sight of the state capital impressed him more than his subsequent visits to Paris and Constantinople.

To reach Schenectady required a stagecoach ride over bad roads though "an almost sterile plain, without culture or dwellings" except for taverns.

The first time he rose to speak the other students laughed at him. Seward discovered that he had a farm boy's "measured drawl." Furthermore, the more elite students considered his clothing crude and inferior. He immediately made a successful effort to refine his accent. The matter of his dress "was only surmounted by my early falling into debt to the accomplished tailors of Schenectady."

His studies went well and he became a popular man on campus through his participation in literary and debate events. But he spent more money than Samuel Seward was sending him. The boy's bills inevitably came to the attention of his father and the two had a serious row. "He declined to pay for my bills that he thought unreasonable," Seward wrote, "and I could not submit to the shame of credit impaired."

So he ran away. In early 1819, in the middle of his final year of college, he slipped out of Schenectady with a friend who was going to teach school in Georgia. He ducked as the stagecoach passed towns where his father was known.

Running away was something of a rite of passage in the Seward household. Three years earlier, his oldest brother had stomped off to Illinois after arguing with his father. The next oldest joined the army rather than endure the patriarch's demands.

As young Seward waited for the schooner to sail, he found time to take in a play at the only theater in New York City. "My first act of dissipation," he called it. He bought the cheapest ticket, 25 cents, and took his seat "taking no notice of my surroundings." At the end of the tragedy's first act he saw men and women in the opposite gallery sneering and laughing at him. A black man sitting nearby quietly explained, "Guess young master don't know that he's got into the colored folk's part of the gallery."

It was enough "to awaken my distrust of my ability to begin the world alone," he wrote.

He had more doubts the following day when the ship got under way in rough seas and "(I) paid the tribute which the ocean exacts of every navigator on his first voyage."

The cold, stormy trip with "few conveniences and no luxuries" lasted a week before the ship docked in Savannah. He traveled to the northwestern part of Georgia by stagecoach, farm wagons and on foot, reaching the settlement of Eatonton flat broke. "With only 18 pence in my pocket, a thousand miles from home … what could I do?"

The 17 year old northerner was accepted by the worthies of the town with open arms and offered the position of superintendent — and probably the only teacher — in an academy still under construction. The job paid $800 a year.

The area, he wrote, had "recently been recovered from the Indians."

He experienced no disdain over his New York roots, but he did note two deep-set prejudices among Eatontonians. One was a dislike of "the lower class of adventurers from the North, called 'Yankees.'" The other "was a suspicion, amounting to hatred, of all emancipated persons, or free negroes, as they were called."

As he waited for Union Academy to be built, a letter from his father arrived. Samuel Seward had searched high and low, walking the docks of New York to get information about a short, red-haired lad who might have been looking for passage to somewhere remote. "He implored me to return," Seward wrote, "and informed me that I would be supplied with what funds I should need."

Seward responded that he liked where he was. But the trustees of the academy received a second letter in which the elder Seward threaten to "prosecute them with the utmost rigor of the law."

Then came pleading letters from his mother and sister. Chastened, the prodigal son found a replacement to accept the job and took his leave.

At the time of this adventure, on the other side of the world, Alexander Baranov left Russian America.

Against all odds, he had turned a ramshackle sprinkling of cabins into a small but stable colony at the far edge of the Russian Empire. He had achieved it through ruthlessness, violence and bare-knuckle business demands extracted from Americans, British, Spaniards, Hawaiians and the obstructionist bureaucracy in St. Petersburg, then Russia's capital.

Katlian and other Tlingit chiefs were guests of honor at his parting dinner. The food was served on china. By this time almost everyone in New Archangel ate food served on Chinese porcelain. In New York, Seward later remarked, most people still used pewter dishes.

Baranov, in his 70s, would not cash in on his years of labor. He died in the Dutch West Indies on the journey back to Russia and was buried at sea.

Seward's voyage home, on the other hand, was pleasant and invigorating. It seems to have sparked a lifelong love of travel. The lure of the sea, he wrote, "took possession of me."

When he returned to Union College for his final semester he found the student body bitterly divided between Northerners and Southerners over the question of whether or not slavery would be allowed in the potential states west of the Mississippi River.

Missouri's application for statehood bounced between the two houses of Congress for two years before a compromise was reached that let Missouri join the Union with its slaves, balanced by the admission of Maine as a free state.

The Missouri Compromise attempted to solve the conundrum of how a nation dedicated to individual liberty could also tolerate humans as property. It successfully postponed for another generation the problem of resolving the conflict. But it could not prevent the inevitable clash unwittingly created by the founders of the nation.

One of those founders, old Thomas Jefferson, former President and slave owner, saw it clearly. The news struck him like a fire alarm in the night as he realized there would be no gentle reconciliation. There must ultimately, he was sure, be a war.

Seward, on the other hand, was a born optimist. Graduating at the top of his class, he gave the commencement speech on the topic of "The Integrity of the American Union." While the republics of history had been short-lived, the United States had the resources of a continent waiting for it and would be permanent, he said. The commerce and genius of America would eventually reach every part of the world by "a thousand sails."

His fellow students weren't so confident. After receiving their diplomas on the stage, those from the North and South departed in two groups and did not speak to one another — an omen of things to come.

Four: Into Politics

Upon graduation Seward returned to Goshen to study law. He decided not to settle there, however, saying he was not fond of the place. Did memories of his boyhood beatings remain too painful?

He passed the bar in 1822 and moved to Auburn, a little town near the Great Lakes. The growing area offered opportunities. It was the location of a grand new state prison, very convenient for one in the legal profession. And it was far from his father.

But his main reason for the move was Frances Miller, a school friend of his sister. Seward enjoyed the company of women, particularly intelligent and educated ones. Frances was both as well as pious, which Seward was not.

Moreover, her father was Elijah Miller, a wealthy judge whose only heirs were his two daughters. Seward had been interested in another woman, he told Samuel. Her father was even wealthier than Judge Miller, but he had seven children. Money, plainly, was a factor when he switched his affections. He was employed by the judge and applied his charm on Frances.

"Eventually intercourse led to marriage," he wrote in his autobiography. Judge Miller gave his consent as long as the couple agreed to live in his house with him.

Mutual respect rather than romantic love may be what kept them together. Seward conferred with Frances on issues of the day and to a great extent she served as his conscience. But his treatment of her often seemed dispassionate.

His true passion was politics. He relished debates and civic activities. He joined the local militia and was among the men who escorted the Marquis de Lafayette on the Revolutionary War hero's tour through the country in 1825.

Young America reveled in partisan activity with an obsession reserved for professional football nowadays, and national politics took a back seat to local and state elections. The hard boundaries of two parties dividing all government between them had not yet been set. A rash of interests, baffling to students of modern campaigns, formed and dissolved coalitions constantly, and these coalitions varied from state to state.

Seward originally sided with the Republican-Democrats of Thomas Jefferson, his father's preference, and opposed the Federalists, John Adams' party.

Those committed to the old Federalist view of things felt public money should be spent on infrastructure. In New York their leader was Governor DeWitt Clinton. His agenda included a canal linking the Hudson River to the Great Lakes.

While in college, Seward wrote an essay explaining that the Erie Canal was an engineering folly that would bankrupt the state. But when the project was completed unprecedented prosperity followed. Seward could see that the canal not only improved the economy, it brought people together. He became a supporter of Clinton and even made fun of his own previous skepticism about the canal.

The Clintonians received a peculiar boost in 1826 when a disaffected member of the Masonic Order, William Morgan, wrote a book revealing the group's secrets.

The Masons were a powerful group of wealthier men whose decisions, made in secret, had great sway on public affairs. Some of them took advantage of their status to have Morgan arrested. He was taken to a remote cell from which he disappeared, never to be seen again. In the course of the investigation it became clear that ranking Masons with political power were covering up for the crimes of their brothers.

Today it seems preposterous that opposition to what most Americans consider a fraternal club could turn into a political movement. But the Morgan case roused widespread indignation. It seemed to confirm what working men and toiling farmers had suspected, that a clandestine clique of elites was keeping them down. The Masons were seen as the new aristocrats. If the Republic were to be saved for the average citizen, their power had to be checked.

Thus the Anti-Masonic Party was born. Seward was friendly toward the cause, though he held back from joining it for a while.

But in 1828 Andrew Jackson was elected President, defeating Seward's preferred candidate, John Quincy Adams. The victory of the Jacksonians, who took the name Democrats, shattered both the old Federalist alliances and Jefferson's coalition, which fed the

Anti-Masons. The party may have sprung from a single issue, but it became the home for anyone who differed with Jackson on a range of economic issues — taxes, tariffs, banking.

Seward became a spokesman for the Anti-Masonic cause. He was asked to stand for the United States House of Representatives but declined, sensing that such a run would be futile at that time. In 1830, however, he ran for the New York state Senate as the candidate of an Anti-Masonic-allied group called the Workingmen Party. With help from his lifelong friend Thurlow Weed, publisher of the influential *Albany Evening Journal* and a shrewd political analyst, he won.

The young man from Auburn made a positive impression upon his colleagues, even those who didn't like his political views. He had a knack for befriending those who had different opinions, always ready to hear their side of things but quick to dispute when he saw a logical weakness in their arguments, then move on with no hard feelings.

His issues included prison reform. He championed the idea of separate jails for women and an end of physical punishments that often amounted to torture. With the help of Democrats, he passed a bill ending imprisonment for debt.

Frances approved of such high-minded goals. But she did not like the bustle of the capital and stayed home. Nor did she like his long absences. No matter. He loved being a public figure and his wife would just have to come to terms with the man she'd married.

If it had been only his occupation that took him away, she might have felt better about it. But he was forever traveling, and not just on political business. In 1833 Samuel Seward decided it was time to see Europe and William eagerly joined him. It took 18 days to sail across the Atlantic and a month to return. Both men, as fond of history as they were of cigars, enjoyed the tour greatly.

Five: A Born Gambler

The dissolution of the Federalists became complete with Jackson's reelection in 1832. From its fragments and outsider groups created over the years a new coalition was formed called the Whigs. The fuss over the Masons had died down and Seward easily stepped into the new party.

"Politicians of the Seward stripe … ride waves of dubious social value," writes biographer Glendon G. Van Deusen. "Once convinced that (a cause) has outlived its usefulness, they abandon it without reluctance."

That did not make Seward a cynic, Van Deusen argues. He had "a real desire to serve the people, to make the country a better place." But it's evident that political power also fed his self-esteem. Such personalities are "gamblers by instinct," Van Deusen writes. "They are fascinated by the element of chance in a political contest."

Chance went against him in 1834 when the Whigs held their first New York convention and put him up as their candidate for Governor. Although he had shown himself to be an able legislator, many were offended by his reformist tendencies, particularly his undisguised sympathy for immigrants. And there were rumors that he was friendly with abolitionists.

Slavery in New York had stopped in 1827. But those who argued too stridently for a complete end to it throughout the country were largely considered to be equivalent to anarchists, somewhat loony and disruptive to the peace and good order of society.

It didn't help that the state's economy slumped. Capital was hard to get. Businesses were shutting. Land sellers were foreclosing on farms. Members of the Workingmen constituency saw their lives getting harder and blamed the people they'd elected. Seward didn't even carry his home county as he went down to defeat.

Out of office, he turned to real estate, managing vast areas where farmers had fallen into arrears, doing what he could to restructure their debts and help them keep their land. He wasn't always successful, but his attention to their plight earned him goodwill that would benefit him in future elections.

He also tried to make up for his neglect of Frances. During his time in Albany she had found comfort in their circle of friends at home. Among them was Albert Tracy, a close associate and backer of Seward's political ambitions. They shared conversations, warm letters and, it appears, a meeting of the minds.

At some point Frances became alarmed. Tracy had said or implied something that is not recorded in the letters that survive. It tormented Frances that she had been inclined to respond. She blurted out her "foolishness" in a letter to her distant spouse.

Today we would say Frances and Tracy had an emotional affair, one that never became physical. But Frances' confession shocked Seward into taking action. He distanced himself from Tracy and started paying more attention to his wife.

However, like many husbands, he did it in a way she didn't particularly want. He decided that they would take a long trip to the South in the summer of 1835 — with just a bit of business on the side. Like paying a call on President Jackson. Seward disagreed with most of Old Hickory's policies, but supported his firm stand in the Nullification Crisis of 1832, when South Carolina had threatened to secede and Jackson had threatened to personally lead an army against them if they did.

The couple rode into Virginia, visited George Washington's home at Mount Vernon and Thomas Jefferson's grave at Monticello. The roads became increasingly bumpy and muddy. Frances endured it until she saw a cluster of black children being maltreated by a slave driver. The idea of going another mile into slave country was too much for her. The couple returned to Auburn and Seward resumed his law practice and land business, juggling political appearances whenever they looked like an investment in the future.

The future came quickly. In 1836 a handful of American adventurers led by Sam Houston defeated the Mexican Army and declared independence for Texas. Suddenly the United States had a new nation on its border, one that rocked the delicate balance of the Missouri Compromise.

Mexico outlawed slavery. It was the main grievance Texan planters had against their adopted country. As its own nation, Texas embraced slave labor. But it was clear that the Lone Star Republic could not sustain itself economically. Sooner or later it would have to ask to join the Union and the power of the slave states would grow.

The Texas question became the "elephant in the living room" for both those who sought to restrict slavery and those who wanted to ensure its continuation and expansion.

The United States, like Texas, was in economic trouble. Andrew Jackson had dissolved the Second Bank of the United States, a move opposed by Seward and other Whigs. Federal funds were re-deposited with smaller banks, many run by Jackson supporters. With little oversight or inspection, they loaned money on ventures that began to fail. By 1837 the nation was in a financial panic. The voters blamed the party in power, the Democrats. Things were looking good if you were a Whig.

Seward couldn't revel in the situation. In January of that year his daughter Cornelia died of smallpox. Shortly after that he was baptized in the Episcopal Church in Westfield, New York. That summer, in a speech on education, he made a strong argument for better schools for girls.

1837 is also the year that the first school for girls opened in New Archangel (now Sitka). Russian hunters had married Native Alaskans, creating a creole population with ties to both the Tsar and their indigenous relatives. They spoke Russian and Tlingit and Alutiiq. They went to St. Petersburg and studied at universities before coming home. They were forming an educated core group in Russia's American colony.

In many ways, the average citizen of New Archangel or Kodiak lived as well or better than the average citizen of the rural United States. Among other things, their children did not die of smallpox. The Tsar's government saw to it that Russian Orthodox clergy and agents of the Russian-American Company administered smallpox vaccine not only in the larger settlements but in the small villages along the Aleutian chain.

But Russian Americans did not have the one blessing that U.S. citizens held above all others, the right that made them kings, the right to vote.

The electorate gave New York Whigs a landslide victory in 1838. Seward became Governor by a respectable margin of 10,000 votes.

Six: Governor Seward

Seward took office with a glorious vision of the future. "Our race is ordained to reach, on this continent, a higher level of social perfection than it has ever yet attained," he said in his first message to the state legislature.

His program included expanding railroads and canals, welcoming immigrants and reforming the civil service. State employees had been paid through the fees they collected; Seward insisted that they should be paid a salary.

The federal Fugitive Slave Act obliged states to return runaway slaves to their masters without a trial. Seward insisted that accused blacks would have their day in court and New York district attorneys would have to convict them before turning them over to their accusers.

Prison reform remained important. In a memoir titled "The Adventures of a Haunted Convict," Austin Reed, a black inmate in the Auburn prison, praised the Governor for letting prisoners have books and credited him for easing the lot of the men behind bars. Seward created an uproar when he ordered that a condemned Catholic awaiting execution be allowed a visit by a priest.

Prejudice against Catholics, especially Irish, was perhaps more intense in New York than prejudice against blacks. Religious instruction was part of every elementary school curriculum and the New York school system was run by a committee that deemed the only doctrine taught would be Protestant, with a good measure of virulent anti-Catholicism thrown in.

Irish immigrants balked at sending their children to such schools and, as a result, many children of Irish parents didn't attend school at all. Seward's efforts to see that educational funding was shared with Catholic schools raised the ire of the anti-immigrant party that took the name "Know-Nothings."

He got his first taste of diplomacy when Alexander McLeod, a

Canadian, was charged with participating in an attack in New York waters on an American ship that had been hired by rebels against the government of Canada. People died in the fighting and witnesses said McLeod boasted of his role in the incident. He was arrested on the American side of Lake Erie and tried for murder.

The British government pressured U.S. Secretary of State Daniel Webster to intervene, but Seward insisted that McLeod be tried in state court. The witnesses against McLeod were not very credible and the accused had a good alibi. The British were mollified and Webster was relieved by his acquittal. Seward also embraced the verdict as a vindication of his state, himself and the rule of law.

Throughout his life, Seward looked back with particular pleasure on his brief term as New York's chief executive. Those who wanted to get on his good side always called him "Governor," even after he had served in high federal offices.

But in 1841 he decided not to run again. Recession had returned and now the Whigs were blamed. His promotion of candidates for government jobs stirred bad blood among those who thought they should have been the choice. And his pro-Irish sympathies infuriated the Know-Nothings.

His favored candidate for Governor lost to Democrat William C. Bouck. Seward took it calmly and then did something no one had ever done before. He attended the inauguration of his successor, listened to his speech and, when it was over, shook Bouck's hand and wished him well.

He returned to Auburn, much to Frances' satisfaction. She never liked the social excitement of Albany and especially disliked the lavish dinners and parties Governor Seward threw to help lubricate passage of his policies.

Those dinners cost much more than the state was willing to pay and Seward suffered some serious business reversals during his term. He resumed his law practice with personal debts of $400,000, around $9 million in 2015 dollars.

Seven: Out of Office

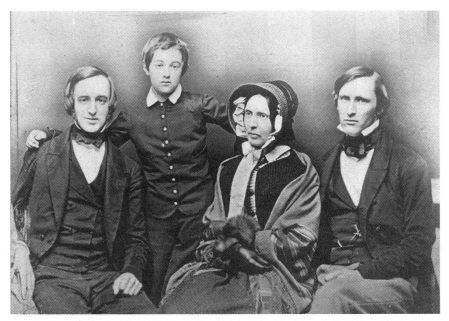

Frances Seward and her sons, Frederick, left, William Jr. and Augustus.
From the collection of the Seward House Museum, Auburn NY.

Bad times caused many Americans to look west. There was said to be good land along the Columbia River. Families gathered their possessions and made the long, dangerous trek to Oregon country. The British thought of it as theirs, but they couldn't populate it. The Willamette Valley soon became an enclave of the United States.

One of those who made the journey to Oregon, a Swiss immigrant named John Sutter, moved south to California. The Russian-American Company had wiped out the sea otters of the California coast and were getting food from the Hudson's Bay Company. They didn't need Fort Ross any more, so they sold it to Sutter in 1841.

Sutter accommodated the increasing flow of American economic refugees whose numbers soon equalled those of Spanish-speaking Californians.

Meanwhile, in Auburn, Seward scrambled to keep his head above water, taking every job that came his way. He had one son, Augustus, at West Point and another, Frederick, preparing to go to college. A third, William Jr., was thought to be too goofy to become a success. And, at the end of 1844, a new baby daughter arrived named Frances, like her mother, but forever known as Fanny. He could not afford to stop working.

Court watching was popular entertainment in those days. Locals packed the galleries to cheer the redemption of the innocent and savor the remorse of the convicted. Out-of-town visitors often stopped in to see the show.

One such out-of-towner was James Wilson. He watched Seward's animated defense of a client and decided this was the attorney he needed for patent infringement cases he was facing. Seward protested that he had no knowledge of patent law, but Wilson made it worth his while to study up on it.

Wilson's patent involved a machine for making planks. Before then, people said, it was easier to shape a log than get a board, especially on the frontier. Even fine homes used square-cut logs for their frame and walls. Wilson's machine did for lumber what Henry Ford's assembly line would later do for automobiles — it caused the price to drop, making finished wood products affordable to an enormous market. But there were plenty of mechanically minded people who could look at Wilson's invention, see how it worked and replicate it.

Seward knocked down the infringers one by one. He proved to be adept at patent law and it made him rich enough to pay off his debts. Soon other inventors were calling for him, including Samuel Morse, whose telegraph wires had begun to connect city to city, and Erastus Corning, whose iron works prospered as railroads expanded.

The 1840s were a time of technological miracles. For the first time in human history messages and cargo moved faster than the speed of a horse. Communication over hundreds of miles could happen in a minute. Journeys that had once taken a week were accomplished overnight.

Seward made use of steamboats, trains and telegraphs as he argued cases from Cincinnati, Ohio to Charleston, South Carolina. The travel gave him an intimate knowledge of the country, its assets, aspirations and attitudes. He loved what he saw of America and couldn't understand how anyone would think otherwise. "The union exists because it is inevitable," he said.

Slavery troubled him, however, not just for moral reasons but because of what he considered its impracticality. He was convinced that free labor must always outperform forced labor. Things like the telegraph, railroads and plank-making machines did not come from bondsmen driven to physical exhaustion by beatings, but only from those with the liberty and leisure to employ their brains. "Power can never permanently reside in a community where slavery exists," he said.

Yet he insisted that there was no reason to use force to end forced labor. The practice would become economically unsustainable in time and vanish quietly. That transformation would happen sooner, rather than later, if only slavery could be kept from spreading outside the states that still had it.

Letting Texas into the Union vastly expanded slave territory, and thus Seward objected to it. But public opinion was with the Texans. Mexican troops regularly waged war on the Lone Star Republic, though they failed to reclaim the region, and the Texans pleaded for the protection of the United States.

Texas was a key issue in the presidential election of 1844. Henry Clay, the Kentucky Senator who battled to keep Northern and Southern interests balanced and the country intact, opposed admitting Texas to the United States. James Polk, an ardent expansionist, was eager to bring it in.

To win the big Northern states of New York and Pennsylvania, Clay positioned himself as the pro-immigration candidate, hoping to obtain the support of German and Irish newcomers who tended to vote Democratic. It backfired. Anti-immigrant riots broke out in Philadelphia, the City of Brotherly Love. The Know-Nothings backed Martin Van Buren, an unabashed nativist. Clay lost New York and Polk won the election.

"The Know-Nothing movement was to me a source of apprehension," Seward said. "When I saw not only individuals but whole communities and parties swept away by an impulse contradicting the very fundamental idea on which the Government rests, I began to doubt whether the American people had such wisdom as I had always given them credit for."

Polk's inauguration was still pending when Texas was annexed. Before he'd been in office a year it became a state. Mexico broke off diplomatic relations and Americans broke into war fever.

The prospect of a war was the most exciting thing in the life of young Jefferson Columbus Davis, a teenager on a farm near Charleston,

Indiana. The man who would one day govern Alaska was at that time a slacker, indifferent to his studies, inclined to daydreams of becoming a polar explorer. Killing Mexicans sounded like an adventure.

When Mexico and the United States came to blows over the Texas border, Davis signed up and saw combat in the Battle of Buena Vista. General Zachary Taylor's victory against a Mexican force three times the size of his own brought him national acclaim. It brought fame to Colonel Jefferson Finis Davis, commander of the Mississippi Rifles infantry regiment, later U.S. Senator and then President of the Confederate States of America. And it brought a promotion for Private Jef Davis of Indiana. Jef, as he signed himself, had discovered he liked military life.

Seward disapproved of the war, but he kept his opinions to himself. In time of war, he said, it was folly for any politician to oppose his country. Instead he stuck with the law business. It wasn't always for the money.

In 1846, he undertook the most impossible case of his life. William Freeman, a black man recently released from prison, had killed a well-liked farmer, his wife, child and mother-in-law. Authorities were barely able to keep a mob from storming the jail and lynching the accused. At his arraignment the courtroom was jammed by spectators who were one and all revulsed by Freeman, by his person as much as his actions.

Prison beatings had left Freeman mad and unable to hear. He laughed and cackled and uttered nonsense replies to questions put to him by the court. The lawyers of Auburn wanted nothing to do with him. Will no one defend this man? asked the judge. A long silence followed.

Then Seward spoke out loudly. "I shall remain counsel for the prisoner until his death!"

If he didn't hear the hiss from his fellow citizens at that moment he certainly felt it in the weeks to come. They were not especially prejudiced by the standards of the day. Nor were they unaware of the anti-slavery sympathies of Auburn's most famous resident and his wife. It would eventually be a matter of public record that the Sewards helped abolitionist Harriet Tubman acquire land two miles from their house where she built a hospital and old folks home. More than a few neighbors must have known that a converted kitchen in the basement of the Seward house was a stop for fleeing slaves on the Underground Railroad and that the former Governor was actively involved in flouting federal fugitive slave laws.

That much they could tolerate and even approve of. But the gruesome Freeman murders sent a shudder through the community that made even enlightened people demand vengeance.

Vengeance would come, but not before Seward had done everything he could to get justice for the accused. He spent several weeks on the investigation before bringing what is cited as the first defense using the plea of innocent by reason of insanity.

It had been shown that Freeman was incapable of understanding his actions, Seward argued. No white person in such a mental state would have been brought to trial. A black man deserved the same treatment. It was an affront to humanity for him to be on trial for his life. "I am not the prisoner's lawyer," he said. "I am the lawyer for society, for mankind."

Seward wrapped up his closing argument with a curious image. He told the jury he knew his defense of Freeman had roused bitterness against him, but he unapologetically reminded them that he would continue to live among them and eventually be buried in Auburn. They could choose to spurn his grave, if they wished. But the time would come when a lone exile, Indian or Negro would pass by his remains and erect over them the epitaph "He was faithful."

The defendant was found guilty and condemned to death. The verdict was reversed on appeal. Freeman died in prison awaiting what likely would have been another conviction, oblivious to anything except his own illness and pain. Seward repeatedly visited him until his death.

The case made headlines throughout the country. Seward's final summation was reprinted far and wide. It would take years for some in Auburn to forgive him. But the Freeman defense gave Seward a national reputation as a brilliant intellect, a man of conscience, a man not afraid to speak boldly on behalf of those without a voice.

Eight: To the Senate

Though Seward privately opposed the Mexican War, he publicly praised the victories at Buena Vista and elsewhere. At the same time he mocked the idea of fighting a war to gain more land. The country already had enough "useless territory," he said.

The war ended with the Treaty of Guadalupe Hidalgo, signed February 2, 1848. It required Mexico to sell 525,000 square miles of its territory north of El Paso for $15 million. The Mexican Cession included the long Pacific coast of Alta California. There, one week before the treaty was signed, a carpenter building a water-powered sawmill for John Sutter spotted gold flakes in the stream.

News of the discovery overrode any lingering dissent concerning the war. In the next seven years 300,000 or more Americans made their way to the gold fields. The small population of Spanish speakers was marginalized.

For the estimated 150,000 Native Americans in California what followed was cataclysmic. The Spaniards and Mexicans had been harsh masters, but they needed the Indians for labor. Mission settlements took up a tiny area and tribes outside their reach traded or defended themselves ably and retained their independence.

The Americans arrived well-armed and distrustful or hateful of Indians. With the sanction of the courts, the U.S. Army joined with vigilante groups in campaigns of extermination. Within 30 years only 30,000 California Indians remained.

What some call the California Genocide was of small concern for the majority of the country. Slavery, on the other hand, was growing in importance.

Seward's views on slavery fell in line with those of many Northern politicians, including a Congressman from Illinois, Abraham Lincoln. These men personally opposed it on both moral and practical grounds. But they felt it would be unconstitutional to force its end in states where it was established.

Seward argued that it would be better for the slaveowners to voluntarily free their forced laborers and be paid for the loss. The end of slavery, he insisted, would be "constitutional, lawful and peaceful."

This was not enough to satisfy the more radical abolitionists, who insisted the practice end immediately, with gunfire if necessary. But Seward's position was too much for slavery supporters. They painted him as the chief spokesman for Northern oppression, an incendiary who wanted a bloody slave insurrection.

By 1848 New York Whigs controlled the state legislature and the governorship. Seward, who had helped campaign for the party, was made a U.S. Senator. He took office in March of 1849 at the same time that Zachary Taylor, the hero of Buena Vista, was sworn in as President.

Taylor owned slaves, but he opposed the expansion of slavery in areas that had been ceded by Mexico. He knew the arid Southwest would not support crops like cotton and sugar that depended on slave labor. But he also felt as Seward did, that any change in the balance of slave and free states could lead to a civil war, and Taylor had seen enough of killing in his military career.

He, too, had opposed war with Mexico, though he fought like a mother bear when ordered to. For both Taylor and Seward, loyalty to the Union counted above all else.

Seward campaigned hard for Taylor in New York, and New York's 36 electoral votes propelled the General into the White House. As a result, Seward had Taylor's ear, which was important when it came to what, for most politicians, was the most important decision of the day — the distribution of lucrative federal offices in New York State.

But Taylor's Vice President, Millard Fillmore, was also a New Yorker. New York Whigs were divided between those beholden to Fillmore and those beholden to Seward. Taylor tended toward Seward's advice, which led to accusations that the New York Senator was manipulating the President or, conversely, that Seward was Taylor's lapdog.

The accusations ended on July 9, 1850, when Taylor died and Fillmore became President, a setback for Seward and perhaps for the country. The crucial issue was not really appointments, but whether new states would be slave or free.

Seward staked out the high moral ground for the anti-slavery cause. His Senate colleagues included some of the most famous names in American history, John Calhoun, Henry Clay, Daniel Webster, Thomas Hart Benton, and the other hero of Buena Vista, Jefferson F. Davis of Mississippi. In early 1850, these worthies were tilting toward the conclusion that the Constitution not only allowed slavery, it forbade federal interference with its expansion.

On March 11 Seward gave a blistering three hour speech in the Senate. "Slavery must give way, and will give way" to economic reality and "to the ripening influences of humanity," he said. He suggested that the fugitive slave laws would be intolerable among Northerners who would recoil at imposing on escaping blacks "a chain that we defy all human power to fasten on ourselves."

As important as the Constitution was, Seward proclaimed, "There is a higher law than the Constitution."

The assertion of a "higher law" infuriated both the advocates of slavery and those who wanted to appease the pro-slavery group. They read it as an attack on the founding fathers and the Republic itself. On the other hand, the speech made him a saint to millions who were coming to the conclusion that slavery was wrong, but had yet to hear a national politician put what they were thinking into words. One hundred thousand copies of the speech were distributed and newspapers everywhere carried long excerpts.

The "higher law" speech had little impact on the immediate — and temporary — solution. Henry Clay's Compromise of 1850 admitted California as a free state, paid Texas $10 million to relinquish its claim on New Mexico and territory north of the Missouri Compromise line, and left the status of the territories of New Mexico and Utah to be decided by the citizens of those regions at a later date.

The compromise also strengthened the fugitive slave laws, which Seward openly condemned and not-so-secretly violated when he hid Harriet Tubman's Underground Railroad "passengers" in his cellar.

Slavery was not his only issue. Convinced that transportation and communication would bind the Union more tightly, Seward advocated for not one, but two railroads across the continent to California, one through the northern part of the country, the other through a southern route. And he pushed for national funding for a trans-Atlantic telegraph cable.

Nine: The Expanding Empire

The benefits of the Mexican Cession became apparent as California gold poured into the national economy. Seward became a tentative supporter of enlarging the nation.

The growth of American agriculture demanded fertilizer and a prime source was found in the deep deposits of bird droppings on remote ocean outcroppings where seabirds nested by the millions. Seward introduced the Guano Islands Bill, claiming for America uninhabited rocks that were unfit for anything, "except for the guano."

The law is still in effect. Johnston Atoll and Midway Island are two possessions America retains under Seward's bill.

In 1852 Seward proposed a naval survey of the Bering Strait region to facilitate the voyages of Yankee whalers who were going into the Arctic Ocean to harvest the whale oil that brightened lamps and oiled the machinery of the booming nation.

The Russians, whose whales were being poached by Yankees, were in no position to protest. The non-Native part of the population was too small to prevent incursions. The Hudson's Bay Company took advantage of Russia's weakness to establish Fort Selkirk on the upper Yukon River and began trading with Athabaskan tribes in the region.

This set off alarms among the Tlingit Indians of the coast, who controlled the passes between the ocean and the interior. They had a monopoly on trade with the interior tribes and realized their economy would shrivel if the Hudson's Bay men had their way.

Koh'klux, a Tlingit leader from the village of Klukwan, near present-day Haines, Alaska, took a war party hundreds of miles over the mountains and surprised the Fort Selkirk interlopers on August 19, 1852, burning the post to the ground.

Koh'klux, also known as Shat-Hitch and other names with various spellings, loomed as large in person as he does in Alaska history. In 1852 he was about 35 years old, a formidable figure, six feet tall, his face scarred from many battles. He once had been shot in the face and survived. He was ready and able to kill anyone who crossed him.

In this case he deemed that humiliation would suffice. After all, the British had killed no one. They had merely interfered with business. There was no need for life-for-life retaliation.

The rattled Hudson's Bay men later boasted about their daring escape on a raft. The Tlingit version is that Koh'klux took their weapons from them, ordered them onto the raft and told them that he wouldn't be so nice if he caught them there again.

Fort Selkirk was not rebuilt for 40 years.

Henry Clay's compromise did not hold up that long. Though the Mexican Cession lands attracted few settlers, except to California, the Great Plains had acquired enough people to make new states possible. The question of whether these states would be free or slave arose again.

Illinois Senator Stephen A. Douglas proposed organizing what was then called the Nebraska Territory, "with or without slavery." Seward objected strenuously, feeling that it would erase the line drawn between slave and free territories by the Missouri Compromise. But the measure passed with the support of many Whigs and President Franklin Pierce.

Kansas soon had two opposing governments, one in Lecompte, which favored slavery, and another in Topeka, which renounced it. Fighting broke out between the anti-slavery forces supplied by supporters in the abolitionist heartland of New England and the Lecompte government reinforced by border-jumpers from Missouri.

The Nebraska-Kansas Bill was legislation nobody liked. The Whigs unraveled over it and so did the Democrats. Pierce, of New Hampshire, hated the idea of abolition, convinced that its advocates were bent on destroying the nation. Northern Democrats abandoned him.

Seward remained a Whig as long as he could, but finally concluded that the party was irrevocably broken, ripped apart by divisions over slavery and immigration.

From displaced Whigs and disaffected Northern Democrats a new party formed, the Republicans. The new party opposed slavery, though it insisted the issue did not merit dissolving the Union. It supported giving or cheaply selling land in the West to homesteaders, a plank of the Free Soil Democrats. And it walked a tightrope with regard to Know-Nothings, saying as little as possible about immigration but resorting to code words like "growth" and "prosperity," agreeable ideas that implied more people would be needed to do more work.

Among those who found a home in the new party were Seward, Lincoln and Senator Charles Sumner, a former Free Soiler from Massachusetts. An ardent abolitionist, Sumner warmed to Seward and became very friendly with Frances. But he was acid-tongued toward his opponents. Even his friend Frances objected to his "cutting personal sarcasm" and Seward agreed with her. Stephen Douglas called him "a damn fool" and wondered aloud how long it would be before "some other damn fool" shot him.

Ten: Prelude to War

Senator Charles Sumner of Massachusetts, who championed the purchase of Alaska even though he was politically hostile to Seward. From the Library of Congress.

The first blows of the Civil War came in May of 1856. Sumner gave a two-day speech dripping with pornographic innuendo and pillorying South Carolina Senator Andrew Butler, comparing him to Don Quixote, infatuated by a harlot.

Two days later, Butler's cousin, Representative Preston Brooks, stalked into the Senate, found Sumner at his desk and demanded an apology. Sumner refused, not even looking up from the paper he was writing on. Brooks used his cane to pummel the Massachusetts Senator nearly to death.

Brooks was exonerated by the House of Representatives. Sumner survived. But the country would never be the same. Southern newspapers praised the attack and wished upon Seward "a double dose."

The Democratic Party refused to renominate Pierce, choosing instead James Buchanan of Pennsylvania, who had little experience in domestic policy. He had served as Secretary of State and minister to Russia and England, two major powers that had been enemies in the Crimean War.

In some sense the Crimean War, 1853-1856, was the first of the world wars. It took place on several fronts. Though the main battle was for the Russian port of Sevastopol on the Black Sea, a British-French fleet also attacked Petropavlovsk on the Kamchatka Peninsula. It was repulsed by a small Russian force and retreated to Victoria, British Columbia. It might have easily taken New Archangel, but the Hudson's Bay and Russian-American companies convinced their respective governments to treat North America as neutral territory.

Twenty years before, the possibility of selling Russian America to the United States had been floated, but dropped. When the Crimean War ended, leaving Russia deeply in debt, the idea came up again. Buchanan, a friend of Russia's, listened to the proposal from ambassador Stoeckl. But further discussions were put on hold as crises at home took the President's attention.

The Mormon majority in Utah Territory was on the verge of armed rebellion. Buchanan asked Congress for money to hire more troops to keep the peace. Republicans, led by Seward, refused, suspecting that he would use the army to support the Lecompte side of the Kansas war. An attempt to buy Cuba for $30 million was similarly shot down because Seward and his political allies felt the island would become another slave state.

In March of 1858 the Supreme Court gave its verdict in the case of Dred Scott, a slave whose master had brought him to a free state. Scott argued that, as an American citizen in a state that did not allow slavery, he ought to be free. The court, however, declared that under the Constitution blacks were not and could never be citizens.

Seward denounced the Dred Scott decision in terms that would be considered impolitic if applied to a Supreme Court decision today. "Judicial usurpation is more odious and intolerable than any other among the manifold practices of tyranny," he said, and argued that it was time to reorganize the judicial branch to bring it "into harmony with the Constitution."

Through all the bitterness of the Kansas-Nebraska debates, the attacks in the press and even from friends, Seward remained personally on good terms with members of the other side, dining, drinking, joking and playing whist with them when they weren't in verbal combat on the floor of the Senate.

He closely cooperated with pro-slave Democrat Texas Senator Thomas Rust and even planned a trip around the world with him. When Rust killed himself in 1857, after being diagnosed with cancer, Seward called it a tragedy for both himself and the country.

In the following year, Mississippi's Jefferson Davis spent weeks in a darkened sickroom because of an eye infection. Seward visited almost every day, reading the newspapers to him and filling him in on the gossip of the capital.

1858 brought an end to the Indian conflicts in the East. The Seminole Nation had firmly resisted relocation to Oklahoma, preferring to hide in the swamps of Florida. Lieutenant Jef Davis, now an artillery officer, was assigned to the Third and final Seminole War. He resented the "inglorious" duty and was relieved when the remnants of the tribe agreed to peace. Davis, under the command of Captain Abner Doubleday, was then ordered to Fort Moultrie, a decrepit depot near Charleston, South Carolina.

The duty was just as boring as Florida, but Davis did have a spell of excitement shortly after his arrival. Doubleday was on leave and Davis was in temporary command when a ship carrying contraband slaves from Africa was apprehended by the U.S. Navy near Cuba. It was brought to Charleston where the crew was indicted for piracy and violating international laws against slaving. The Africans were brought to Fort Moultrie to await transport home.

Certain Charlestonians claimed the Africans were their property. They were backed up by the local courts and the sheriff. A mob threatened to riot and abduct the Africans from crumbling Fort Moultrie. It wouldn't have been hard.

To keep the Africans safe, Davis moved them to Fort Sumter, still under construction on an island in the middle of Charleston Harbor. Davis had no objection to slavery, but he steadfastly refused to turn the refugees over to the Carolinians, despite blistering threats, until another Navy ship arrived to take them back to Africa.

When Davis returned to Charleston, he was met by catcalls and curses. The Lieutenant acted as if he didn't hear them and calmly marched back to his post at Fort Moultrie to resume his duties as assigned.

Eleven: Preparing for the Nomination

Fanny Seward with her father. From U.S. National Archives and Records Administration

By 1859 it became clear that the next President would be from the new, growing and rapidly consolidating Republican Party. Seward and most insiders presumed it would be him. He had the experience, the gravitas and the connections. He had loudly opposed the expansion of slavery and endorsed the expansion of commerce. He had more national name recognition than any other man in the party.

He also had enemies, not the least of whom were the remnants of Millard Fillmore's Know-Nothings who hated him as much as Southern slave owners did.

The Republicans' main money man and organizer, Thurlow Weed, suggested Seward lie low for a while so as not to further inflame hard feelings. Seward always listened to Weed's advice and usually profited from it. He arranged a grand tour of Europe. After all, supporters said, when he's President he'll need to know other heads of state. Furthermore, Weed saw to it that Seward's letters from abroad would be published in newspapers around the country.

A few days before Seward set sail, another transoceanic passenger, Anna Furuhjelm, wrote to her mother "a regular gossiping letter" from aboard the British ship *RMS Trent*. She reported what she had seen while on shore at St. Thomas in the Virgin Islands, then a possession of Denmark. The Government House was "very small and magnificent looking," she wrote. "Ours in Sitka is much larger and handsomer."

Anna was the wife of Hampus Furuhjelm, the recently appointed Governor of Russian America, en route to New Archangel from St. Petersburg via London, the Isthmus of Panama and San Francisco.

Anna Furuhjelm's mother was a Scot. Her letters home give a rare contemporary look at Russian America in English.

(The *Trent*, we shall see, would play an enormous role in Seward's legacy.)

During Seward's two months in Great Britain, English gentry found him a braggart, ignorant and probably an Irish sympathizer. But as the presumed next President of the United States he was greeted with propriety, introduced to political leaders and Queen Victoria.

He traveled to the continent, ultimately to Jerusalem, returning by Italy, where he met Pope Pius IX, and to France, where he had an audience with dictator Napoleon III. He took in the sights, talked with prominent intellectuals and kept up with the news from home, which arrived at least two weeks after the fact.

In November he learned of John Brown's raid on the federal weapons depot at Harper's Ferry, Virginia the month before. Brown, a veteran of the fighting in "Bleeding Kansas," hoped to incite and equip a slave rebellion in the South. A few of his meager company managed to flee to safety as U.S. soldiers retook the depot. But most were killed or, like Brown, captured.

Seward professed not to be disturbed by the putsch, but he realized it was time to get home. He arrived in Auburn in late December, three weeks after Brown was hanged, and quickly went into campaign mode with speeches lambasting both slavery and Brown.

The Democrats' convention was a disaster. Southerners walked out and selected their own candidate, John Breckenridge, Buchanan's Vice President. The remaining delegates split their choices still further, most going with Stephen Douglas of Illinois.

Douglas had won the 1858 election for U.S. Senate by defeating Abraham Lincoln in a campaign marked by a series of debates that made Lincoln nationally famous. His name was put forth as a presidential nominee, but Weed and other party leaders outside Illinois considered him to be a small-time country lawyer.

Other contenders included adamant abolitionist Governor Salmon Chase of Ohio and the more conciliatory Edward Bates of Missouri. But Seward was confident. As the Republican convention started in Chicago he had more delegates than anyone else.

However, he did not have quite enough delegates to claim the nomination on the first ballot. Bates' and Chase's supporters, seeing their candidates had no chance, started cutting deals. Lincoln's friends chipped away at the wavering delegates.

Lincoln waited nervously in Springfield, Illinois for word from the convention. Seward sat in his garden in Auburn chatting with friends as the day wore on. He was sitting there when a telegraph arrived with the news, "Lincoln nominated third ballot."

It was a soul-crushing defeat. Yet he spoke calmly. "Mr. Lincoln will be elected and has some of the qualities to make a good president," he said.

Twelve: Campaigning for Lincoln

Condolences poured in from Seward's colleagues, from Charles Francis Adams, the son of John Quincy Adams, and Jefferson Davis of Mississippi.

"His friends feel much distress," wrote Fanny in her diary. "He alone has a smile. He takes it with philosophical and unselfish coolness."

Seward tried to sidetrack his pain by analyzing what had gone wrong.

Lincoln had played his cards brilliantly. Weed and Seward focused on the national election; Lincoln focused on the convention. The trip to Europe had been a mistake. While Seward was sizing up Napoleon III, Lincoln had been hustling for delegates. The convention's setting in Chicago worked to the benefit of the candidate from Illinois. And Seward's former ally, publisher Horace Greeley, had turned on him for not being sufficiently anti-slavery.

Most of all, the Know-Nothings had vented their animosity toward Seward's pro-immigrant stance. In fact Lincoln was as pro-immigrant as Seward. They also held almost identical views on the question of slavery. Both wanted it to end, but not violently. Both thought that whether freed blacks voted was up to the individual states. Neither felt that blacks and whites could live together in harmony, any more than either thought whites and Indians could coexist. Lincoln was of the opinion that, just as eastern Indians had mostly been deported to the west side of the Mississippi River, the best option regarding slaves was to send them all back to Africa.

Lincoln, however, kept some of his opinions under wraps. He was not the lightning rod that Seward might have been. Greeley could support him. Know-Nothings could support him. Moderates could support him. Seward observed, "In an election you must put forward the man who will carry the highest number of votes." The convention determined that man was Lincoln and, Seward later professed, "We have never had reason to regret it."

Both men also felt that preserving the Union was the important thing. Friends who had met Lincoln assured Seward that the Illinoisan was worthy of his support, and perhaps the only man who could keep the country together.

Seward took a few weeks to lick his wounds. Then he hurled himself into campaigning on Lincoln's behalf. He made a "whistle stop" tour, giving speeches in towns from New England to Kansas. He was accompanied by Charles Francis Adams Sr. and his son, Charles Jr., who left a vivid picture of the Senator: "Small, rusty in aspect, dressed in a coat and trousers apparently made 20 years ago and by a bad tailor at that."

Charles Jr.'s brother, historian Henry Adams, famously described Seward as looking like "a wise macaw."

The party traveled by train, paddlewheel steamer and stagecoach. Seward was met by throngs of militant young Republicans who called themselves the "Wide Awakes." He gave stemwinder speeches that enthralled the crowds and awed the reporters who wrote about them. But on the topic of immigration he spoke obliquely, substituting the vision of a mighty growing nation that would fill the continent. The implication was that it would not happen without fresh populations arriving. In Chicago the audience cheered his prediction that America would be, in fact already was, "a new and great empire." Canada would surely join the states and the trading posts of Russian America would "yet be the outposts of my own country."

Lincoln barely won in Illinois, Indiana and Ohio, the states whose electoral votes gave him the majority in the November elections. A number of those votes were Know-Nothings who would have gone for Douglas over Seward but had no problem in supporting the enigmatic Lincoln.

A greater number were moderates who, safe to say, had been influenced by Seward's speeches. Lincoln arguably owed his victory to Seward and both men knew it.

Lincoln offered Seward the position of Secretary of State, saying, "It has been my purpose, from the day of nomination at Chicago, to assign you, by your leave, this place in the administration."

Seward asked for time to consider the offer. He conferred with Weed, who was on his way to Springfield to ascertain Lincoln's intentions. But before Weed could return events began spinning out of control.

On November 7, 1860, as soon as Lincoln's election became known, Jef Davis was ordered to prepare the recently mounted guns at Fort Moultrie for action. For the first time, he grimly recalled, "gun cartridges were issued in anticipation of an armed insurrection."

Thirteen: The Secession Winter

On December 20, 1860, South Carolina seceded from the Union. Fort Moultrie's commander, Captain Robert Anderson, abandoned his vulnerable position and relocated his men to Fort Sumter. Davis brought up the rear, leaving Fort Moultrie after destroying ammunition and anything else of military value.

As the crisis grew, Frances pleaded with her husband to wash his hands of Lincoln's offer. "Thirty-five years of the best part of man's life is all that his country can reasonably expect of him," she wrote.

"I will not decline," he replied. "I will try to save freedom and my country."

His service to his country was never more important than in the four months between Lincoln's election and his inauguration.

The Commander of the Army, General Winfield Scott, warned President Buchanan that there was a serious threat of rebellion and a strong possibility that Washington itself would fall to an attack from the South. He urged sending reinforcements to protect federal forts, armories and property in the slave states, but noted that there were no reinforcements to be had. Congress' refusal to pay for troops in the West had left the nation with a token army.

Buchanan attempted to relieve Fort Sumter by sending an unarmed steamer with troops and supplies. As it entered Charleston Harbor the guns of Fort Moultrie, now in the hands of the South Carolina militia, fired on it. The ship retreated. The soldiers in Fort Sumter counted their rations and realized no further help was coming.

Secessionist action spread quickly from South Carolina. By the end of January, five more states had left the Union and several others were preparing to do so. The outgoing President was paralyzed. The President-elect couldn't be seen to be giving orders before inauguration day. He was in no position to call for an army without looking like a dictator, a name some were already calling him.

Every passing hour made it more likely that armed Southern forces would seize the District of Columbia, the Capitol and federal offices in a single march.

Seward took it on himself to make sure that there would be a country by the time Lincoln took the oath of office in March. By now it was known that he would be the next Secretary of State, the highest post in the Cabinet. Relying on that, his position in the Senate and his connections in the Republican Party, he contacted Northern governors and convinced them to raise state militias to protect Washington. He demanded that New York bankers lower the interest they were charging on money they loaned to the government. He got secret intelligence from inside the Buchanan Cabinet smuggled to him by clandestine couriers. In unguarded moments he wished for an invasion by Britain or France to unite the country against a common enemy.

Privately, he now felt war was certain. But in public he continued to be calm and positive. He supported calls for a constitutional convention to address slavery and a peace conference to defuse the possibility of conflict. There was still cause for hope. Missouri, Tennessee, Kentucky and Virginia all had strong Union partisans. As long as Seward could keep them talking, there might be no fighting.

Within his own party some were already calling for an all-out attack on South Carolina. But that would cause the South to unite and incite the border states to join them. Besides, the North as yet had no army.

On the other hand a conciliatory movement was underway in the Senate to soothe the South by guaranteeing the right to own slaves. Seward himself intimated that Fort Sumter would shortly be surrendered with no hard feelings.

Surely he didn't believe it, and neither did his opponents. But the canard maintained a delicate balance during three months of chaos. The Union did not try to reinforce Fort Sumter and the South Carolinians held their fire. Everyone waited to see what would happen.

On February 13, as federal troops stood guard, the electoral votes were counted and Lincoln was officially declared the next President. "I have brought the ship off the sands," Seward wrote to his wife, "and am ready to resign the helm."

But the pre-inauguration crisis got worse. On February 21, as Lincoln was traveling to Washington, General Scott learned of an attempt to abduct or assassinate him as he passed through Baltimore, a city boiling with pro-secession sentiment.

Scott informed Seward, who sent his son Frederick to warn the President-elect. "Find Mr. Lincoln, wherever he is," he said. "Let no one know your errand."

Frederick managed to intercept Lincoln, who changed his plans, arriving quietly in Washington on the morning of February 23. That night he dined at Seward's house. The next day William Seward introduced the President-elect to key members of Congress.

Lincoln immediately took a liking to Seward. He brought him a draft of his proposed inaugural address. Seward suggested some 200 changes, slight adjustments that made the speech less belligerent. Lincoln adopted most of them when he delivered the address before being sworn in on March 4, 1861.

On the same day the U.S. Senate passed a constitutional amendment that would prohibit federal interference with slavery.

Lincoln had no objection to the amendment as long as it brought back the states that had seceded. Seward had reservations, but found hope in the fact that the amendment at least allowed states to renounce slavery themselves.

The "secession winter" could well have shattered the nation without a shot being fired. That it did not was due to William Seward. Those who wanted to save the Union needed time and, almost single-handedly, he bought it for them. In the opinion of Henry Adams, it "might go down in history as one of the wonders of statesmanship."

Fourteen: The War Begins

A s he took over as Secretary of State, Seward's work had just begun. His first job was to remove the many Southern sympathizers in the State Department and replace them with loyal Unionists. His second duty, with the rest of the Cabinet, was to help the President determine how to avoid bloodshed while asserting federal authority or, if it were impossible to do both, how to prepare for war.

Two military posts seemed key to maintaining order, Fort Sumter and Fort Pickens in Florida. But the Navy could only deploy one ship capable of securing them, the big-gunned steam frigate *Powhatan*. Seward argued that Sumter's position was hopeless and that the warship should be sent to Florida.

Secretary of the Navy Gideon Welles took the opposite view. Pickens was well-prepared for an assault, but Sumter was still under construction. The *Powhatan* could supply cover for tugs bringing in material and reinforcements.

Lincoln agreed with Welles. He would inform South Carolina that ships were coming to resupply the fort but did not intend to cause trouble.

In the confusion of the hour, Lincoln signed orders for the ship to sail to Fort Pickens. When the mistake was discovered, he had Seward send a message to the captain redirecting him to Charleston. The bewildered commander, looking at two contradictory orders, went with the one signed by the ranking officer — the President — and continued to Florida.

Welles was convinced that Seward had done it on purpose, but Lincoln accepted blame for the mistake.

About this time, Seward wrote a long letter to Lincoln known as "Some thoughts for the President's consideration." The exact contents are not known, but upon receiving it Lincoln summoned Seward to the White House and the two had a long talk behind closed doors.

It is presumed that Lincoln commanded the conversation, thanking Seward for his advice, probably agreeing with much of it, but stressing that he, not the Secretary of State, would be the leader of the team trying to save the nation.

It is also likely that at this meeting the two revealed to each other their worst fears, that war was certain. Distasteful as it was, ruthless military action would be necessary to preserve the country. A few days after, the British journalist William Russell, playing whist with Seward, found the Secretary's attitude decidedly "bellicose."

At 4:30 a.m. on April 12, shore batteries began shelling Fort Sumter. Jef Davis' artillery fired back. The siege lasted two days, reducing the fortifications to rubble before the garrison surrendered. A transport ferried the defenders to a U.S. Navy ship waiting offshore.

The battle was over. The war had begun.

Fifteen: The Trent Affair

All hope of peace vanished following the fall of Fort Sumter. Lincoln issued a call for troops and large armies assembled in the North and South.

Virginia ultimately seceded. Arkansas, Tennessee and North Carolina followed. The Confederate forces were led by Robert E. Lee, whom Winfield Scott called the most competent officer he had ever known. The industrial barons of France and Britain pushed their governments to side with the slave owners and keep the supply of cotton coming.

Seward went into overdrive. He vehemently insisted that the conflict would be short, the Union would prevail in a few weeks or months. He also dropped not-so-veiled threats that any nation that aided the South would be next to feel the wrath of the re-United States of America.

Domestic matters were not his department, but Seward concurred with Lincoln's decision to suspend *habeas corpus* and, at his direction, more than 800 alleged Confederate sympathizers were arrested and imprisoned. This left a sour taste with many. No one was more relieved than Seward when Congress backed up the President's policy, passing legislation to square it with the Constitution.

The Union had two strategy options. One was Winfield Scott's plan to cut the Confederacy off from outside support, blockading the ports on the Atlantic Ocean and Gulf of Mexico while securing the Mississippi River. It would be a long and costly operation. But, given the resources of each side, it would assure the North of victory.

The second option was a fast, full-out attack with overwhelming force. More than 30,000 troops protected Washington, D.C., and the capital of the Confederacy, Richmond, Virginia, was only 100 miles away. One quick punch and it could be over with. This plan had the support of the military, public opinion and the majority of the Cabinet.

On July 21, 1861, the Union Army tried a surprise attack on the Confederate positions. Each side had about 18,000 troops on hand and more in reserve, none of whom were particularly well trained. The Union surge failed and the first Battle of Bull Run turned into a chaotic retreat. Only exhaustion kept Lee from overrunning the capital.

Lincoln realized he needed better generals. He asked for suggestions from Seward, who sent a list that included the name of George McClellan. Dashing and charismatic, McClellan seemed like a good choice to buoy morale as well as drill the Northern volunteers into a real fighting force.

But "Fighting Mac" disapproved of the war and detested the politicians he blamed for starting it. He considered Scott "a traitor." Lincoln was a buffoon and Seward "a meddling, officious, incompetent little puppy."

McClellan's feelings were known to the President and the Secretary. Both were getting used to insults. Senator Sumner agreed with McClellan concerning Seward's incompetence. The President's wife, Mary Todd Lincoln, called him an "abolitionist sneak."

Seward couldn't let mere name-calling get to him. He had to deal with the leaders of France and Britain who doubted that the war would be over any time soon. They saw that the South might beat the North if things continued to go as they had at Bull Run.

Seward redoubled his efforts to assure them that the battle was only a skirmish and that events on the ground would soon swing in favor of the Union. It was not an easy sell. Ambassadors from around the world stationed in Washington, D.C. had seen and felt the terror that enveloped the capital as panicked soldiers flooded back from Bull Run.

To influence European opinion Seward sent the so-called "envoys" across the Atlantic. They included his old friends Thurlow Weed, Catholic Archbishop of New York John Hughes and Charles McIlvaine, Episcopal Bishop of Ohio. Their job was to hobnob with the political elites, pick up any tidbits they could and say things that that might be inappropriate coming from the mouths of accredited ambassadors. When McIlvaine, for instance, chatted over tea at Buckingham Palace — and he often did — he was speaking as a private citizen, not as the representative of his country. Seward saw they were suitably funded for their not-so-secret missions, even though their role was technically unofficial.

The official ministers chafed at the presence of the envoys, but they may have done much good. Throughout the grim months of

1861, as the South succeeded in the field, no foreign power took the critical step of recognizing the Confederacy as a nation.

But they came frightfully close.

In November a U.S. warship stopped and boarded the *RMS Trent* en route from Cuba to England. Two Confederate officials were found among the passengers. Former senators John Slidell and James Mason were on their way to represent the secessionist government in France and England. The Americans took both men prisoner. They were incarcerated in Boston.

Northern supporters were jubilant. Two arch-traitors had been captured and would face justice. Praise rained on the captain who had apprehended them.

The English were furious. Under international law, stopping the ship of a neutral country at sea showed belligerence, and forcibly removing persons from such ships was an act of war.

Her Majesty's ambassador demanded the release of Slidell and Mason and set a hard deadline after which diplomatic relations would be terminated. The threat was backed up by actions. Shipments of saltpeter, needed for the manufacture of ammunition, were held up at English ports. Troops were sent to Canada. And, not coincidentally, an expedition of 50,000 British, French and Spanish soldiers invaded Mexico — ostensibly to collect on debts owed by that republic, but a clear violation of the Monroe Doctrine and an insult to the United States.

Ominously, a royal warship waited off the coast of America to take the British minister home if Seward did not give a satisfactory answer by the deadline.

Biographer Walter Stahr calls the *Trent* Affair "the Cuban missile crisis of the 19th century." Most Union partisans felt the arrests were justified. On an emotional level, Lincoln and Seward agreed with them. But the fact was that, even if America were morally right and could match Britain in a land war, superior British sea power would easily plow a path to Southern ports for the export of cotton and the import of weapons.

Seward can be called the man who saved the country in the crisis of the Secession Winter. But in that situation he was aided by many willing partners.

In the *Trent* Affair, however, he stood alone. Neither the military nor political allies nor public opinion could assist him in assuaging Great Britain, which insisted on a plain yes or no answer. His enemies, even as they realized the peril facing the Union, licked their lips, certain that whichever decision the Secretary proposed, it would mean the end of his career.

Submission to British demands would be seen as both capitulation to the Confederacy and buckling to the monarchy that a much younger and weaker America had twice faced down in war. Any show of appeasement would draw the contempt of those fighting for the Union.

But to keep the prisoners would not only dash any hope of co-operation with the most powerful nation on Earth, but force it into declaring war on the United States.

Lincoln was counting on his Secretary of State to find a face-saving way out of the trap. And Seward did not fail him — or the nation.

In the 11th hour he proposed a response that acknowledged British demands while preserving American honor. Ever the lawyer, he framed an argument built on American complaints that had led to the War of 1812. The United States went to war then, he noted, because the English had dragged sailors off American ships. The treaty ending that war stipulated that cases involving the interception of ships at sea would be settled by maritime courts. That particular clause was considered a crowning triumph for American pluck and diplomacy.

The captain had done his duty as he saw it, Seward said, and the Confederate ministers were undoubtedly enemies to be pursued and punished by all legitimate means. However, the law had not been properly followed. The *Trent* itself should have been brought to Boston and the matter turned over to a tribunal consisting of judges from both the United States and England.

Unpleasant as it was, he said, America must remain true to its treaty obligations and the principles for which its soldiers and sailors had bled.

Even those Cabinet members most insistent on rejecting British demands saw no holes in the argument. Lincoln thought about it long and hard before responding "I could not make an argument (against Seward's position) that would satisfy my own mind."

Slidell and Mason were remanded to the British ambassador and allowed to continue to Europe. England stood down. Relief erupted on both sides of the Atlantic. Theaters interrupted performances to announce the news. Crowds gathered and rejoiced that there would be no third Anglo-American war. Attorney General Bates expressed the opinion of many when he said the resolution had preserved "the existence of the nation."

"There are many points at which Seward changed the course of American history," writes Stahl, "but few as momentous as the *Trent* crisis."

The loose ends of the *Trent* Affair, and the War of 1812, were tied up with an agreement that allowed both the United States and Great Britain to search ships at sea for a ten-year period. When it was unanimously ratified by the U.S. Senate, Seward said, "If I have done nothing else, I deem this treaty sufficient to have lived for."

Sixteen: Stanton Joins the Team

Edwin Stanton, Lincoln's Secretary of War, who nursed Seward after his fall from a carriage. Photo from the Library of Congress.

By the beginning of 1862 Lincoln knew he had the wrong man as his Secretary of War. Simon Cameron of Pennsylvania had helped Lincoln receive the nomination in the 1860 election and, it was widely held, received the Cabinet position in exchange. But the war was not going well and Cameron's ideas weren't helping. He proposed, for instance, arming slaves to create an internal rebellion in the South. Seward and Lincoln felt that such an uprising would surely shed the blood of white civilians. An overt race war would cause condemnation abroad, revulsion and backlash in the North. With congressional elections coming up, Lincoln could not afford to alienate national sympathy.

Cameron was asked to become the ambassador to Russia. It was a demotion, but upon realizing that he would either leave the department voluntarily or be fired, he accepted it. In his place Seward suggested Edwin Stanton who, as Buchanan's Attorney General, had covertly cooperated with Seward during the Secession Winter.

Stanton and Lincoln had a history. Stanton had once called Lincoln an "ape." But Seward insisted that Stanton was the man for the job — and Lincoln was not the type to let past insults distract him from the important business of the present. Within days, Stanton was virtually living at the War Department, working with the Commander in Chief and the Secretary of State with a remarkable singleness of mind.

1862 opened well for Jef Davis. He was now a colonel, rapidly rising due to his impressive victories in Missouri. Davis was a rarity in the Union Army, an officer with previous combat experience who had begun his career as a private and advanced entirely on his own merits. On January 2 he married his sweetheart, Marietta Athon. Wasting little time on a honeymoon, he returned to action and had a string of successes that earned him the rank of general in May.

Marietta loved the military as much as her husband and took great pride in being an Army wife.

Frances Seward, on the other hand, resented the role of hostess for her husband. She was exhausted by the pomp and parties of Washington, D.C. She returned to Auburn.

Other members of the family, however, reveled in their father's business. Frederick served as Assistant Secretary of State and wrote a first-hand account of Seward's career. The youngest child, Fanny, still a teenager, spent as much time as she could at the residence on Lafayette Park and left a wonderful fly-on-the-wall diary of what she saw in the Civil War.

In April Britain and Spain withdrew from the Mexican invasion. They had come to realize that Napoleon III's true intention was to make Mexico part of the French Empire. There was still nothing America could do about the matter, but at least now Seward only had to worry about one foreign army, not a coalition. At Seward's urging, Lincoln took no action except to express America's disapproval and extend his best wishes to the nationalist government of Benito Juarez.

Lincoln's great frustration in 1862 was George McClellan. McClellan loved drills and parades. His forces were significantly bigger than those of Robert E. Lee. More than once Lincoln saw opportunities to strike at weak Rebel lines and directed McClellan to attack. Each time, Fighting Mac made excuses or presented only a token response, insisting on more men and more time to prepare them.

Under pressure from Stanton and Lincoln, he finally moved and by May 12 was within striking distance of Richmond. But he couldn't follow up on his success. In the following month Lee counterattacked in the brutal Seven Days Battle, bringing horrific casualties to both sides and sending the bluecoats into retreat.

McClellan's response was to blame his superiors. He snubbed Lincoln and told Stanton, "You have done your best to sacrifice this army."

Again he demanded more soldiers. And again Lincoln agreed. But recruitments were drying up as the war fever of the early days of the conflict cooled. Lincoln did not feel he could take unilateral action.

So the President turned to Seward, who contacted governors of several states and convinced them to petition the President to raise additional troops. Their petition gave the administration political cover and another 300,000 men went into uniform.

Seventeen: Emancipation

The reading of the Emancipation Proclamation by Lincoln to his cabinet as depicted in an engraving by Alexander Hay Ritchie after a painting by Francis Carpenter. Photo from the Library of Congress.

In April of 1862 slaves were freed in Washington, D.C., with compensation paid to their owners. At Seward's direction the State Department began to issue passports that made no reference to the race of the holder, a federal first.

In July Lincoln brought up the possibility of emancipating slaves in the rebellious states. He read a draft of his proclamation to the Cabinet. There was agreement that it was justified both as a humanitarian move and as an act of war. Seward, however, raised questions about the language and the timing. With the string of Union setbacks, he said, issuing the decree now might be read as an act of desperation, "the convulsive struggles of a drowning man."

He advised holding off until the Union could claim a decisive victory. Lincoln concurred and set the proclamation aside. For the next few months he and Seward exchanged drafts tweaking the wording. About a third of the final version was the work of the Secretary of State.

In the painting by Francis Carpenter of Lincoln reading the proclamation to his Cabinet, all eyes are looking at Seward, who is the central figure of the canvas. While everyone, including Lincoln, waits for his reaction, the Secretary seems to be ruminating on the details, the fingers of his right hand positioned on the table like a compass taking the measurements of a map.

His calculations would have included the fact that Europe was getting impatient. France was pushing for third-party arbitration of the war, a move that would have essentially ended the Union. In England William Gladstone declared that the Southern states were, in fact, "a nation."

In September it seemed that Gladstone might be right. At the Second Battle of Bull Run Lee pushed through Union lines and crossed into Maryland.

McClellan was now forced to fight. With twice as many troops as the Confederates he met Lee at the Battle of Antietam. Each side lost more than 12,000 men in what is cited as the single bloodiest day in American history. Lee might have been taken out by the superior Union forces. But McClellan inexplicably disengaged.

Tactically, Antietam was a draw. Strategically, it was the Union win Lincoln had been waiting for to announce his Emancipation Proclamation. The document freed only slaves in territory held by the Rebel states and would be in effect only as long as Lincoln was the Commander in Chief. It was presented to the public as a war measure, not a civil rights law. As Lincoln explained, "My paramount objective is to save the Union and is not to save or destroy slavery."

The proclamation, countersigned by Seward, was published in newspapers around the country on September 23. In the short term it divided the country more than ever. Arguments over war strategy further weakened support for the President's party. So did the suspension of *habeas corpus*, the arrest of civilians and the closing of newspapers that sided with the South, even after Congress approved the measure.

Most controversial of all was Lincoln's decision to sack McClellan. Relieved of his command on October 24, Fighting Mac didn't take it graciously. He resigned from the Army and began planning to challenge Lincoln for the presidency.

The Republicans lost the 1862 elections in a landslide, replaced by Democrats who were mostly pro-Union, but foes of Lincoln. In many quarters, the problems were blamed on the President's closest advisor, Seward. A number of Congressmen and Senators, including Frances Seward's dear friend Charles Sumner, called for his resignation. Secretary of the Treasury Chase encouraged the detractors. Postmaster General Montgomery Blair and Secretary of the Navy Welles, for their own reasons, sided with Chase.

In this poisonous atmosphere, Seward felt that his presence was tying the President's hands and distracting from the war effort. On December 17 he gave his letter of resignation to Lincoln and started boxing up his papers at the State Department.

Lincoln asked Seward to hold off until he could figure out how to keep his Cabinet together. The President didn't trust anyone but Seward to prevent Europe from tilting toward the South. He addressed his concerns to the rest of the Cabinet. Blair agreed that any disagreements could be handled without losing Seward and Welles also switched sides, saying that the Senate shouldn't dictate a President's Cabinet choices.

The matter was resolved when Chase gave Lincoln his own letter of resignation. The President insisted that he needed the talents of both men. A truce, if not out and out peace, was established — for the time being.

Squabbling was the order of the day. Amid the setbacks in combat, loss of public confidence and tension in the Cabinet, infighting swelled among the Union officer corps. Decisions were sometimes tentative, often countermanded. Tempers flared.

General Davis was on sick leave when the Rebel army pushed into Kentucky. He shook off his malaise and returned to duty, assigned to General William "Bull" Nelson.

Nelson was known as a bully. He chastised Davis for no particular reason. Davis showed up at his lodging on September 29 and demanded an apology. Nelson refused. Davis pulled out a gun and shot the unarmed Nelson in cold blood.

Davis admitted to the killing and was placed under arrest.

Confederates in Kentucky were just one of the enemies the U.S. Army faced on its own territory. In August, sensing the disarray in the forces that had oppressed them for so long, the Sioux tribe of Minnesota launched a well-organized attack on settlements, killing 800 whites.

American Indians fought on both sides of the Civil War, but a substantial number wore the gray. Many of them also owned slaves.

Few of them liked men in blue uniforms with guns.

The Sioux were crushed. Some 1,000 warriors were captured. Hundreds were sentenced to death.

It fell to the Great Emancipator to consider clemency. He pardoned many of the Sioux combatants, but upheld the sentences of 38. They were hanged on the day after Christmas of 1862, the largest number of executions in one day in American history.

*William Henry Seward as a young politician. Portrait by Henry Inman from the
collection of the Seward House Museum, Auburn NY.*

Seward as Governor of New York, by Chester Harding from the State of New York.

The "Underground Railroad" room in the basement of the Seward House Museum in Auburn, New York. Escaping slaves are said to have stayed here while en route to Canada. Photo by Michael Dunham.

The carriage in which Seward was riding when he fell to the ground in an attempt to stop runaway horses, suffering life-threatening injuries, remains on display at the Seward House Museum in Auburn, New York. Photo by Michael Dunham.

"Signing the Alaska Treaty," by Emanuel Leutze. Seward is seated on the left and Russian minister Edouard de Stoeckl stands at the globe as translators compare the language of the English and French versions of the treaty. Frederick Seward is shown on the far right along with Senator Charles Sumner of Massachusetts, who was informed of the midnight deal but not actually there. The original is prominently displayed in the dining room of the Seward House Museum in Auburn, New York.
From the collection of the Seward House Museum, Auburn NY.

Seward's study at the Seward House Museum. He died on the green couch on the right of the photo. Photo by Michael Dunham.

The Seward home in Auburn, New York, now the Seward House Museum, as seen from the garden where Seward was waiting in 1860 when word came that Abraham Lincoln had defeated him for the Republican presidential nomination.
Photo by Michael Dunham.

The Seward family plot at Fort Hill Cemetery in Auburn, New York. William Seward's sarcophagus is flanked by those of his daughter Fanny (foreground) and wife Frances. Photo by Michael Dunham.

Eighteen: Gettysburg

Jef Davis got off easier than the Sioux. Nelson had friends in high places, including Secretary of War Stanton, but he had few among his fellow officers. General William Sherman needed the homicidal Davis and interceded on his behalf. The case got moved from civilian to military courts where it was delayed for 30 days, after which, under military law, it had to be dismissed.

Davis went back to the front and resumed scoring wins for the Union. Between battles he wrote letters lashing out at Washington. Hearing of the contretemps with the Cabinet and the possible resignations of Seward and Chase, he chortled, "I for one shall not regret to hear of a total change. It never was a cabinet that could govern the country and secure a peace."

But the Cabinet did not change. If anything, Seward's aboveboard response to the Cabinet cabal drew Lincoln closer to him.

Historian Doris Kearns Goodwin describes in detail the close friendship between the President and the Secretary. Lincoln turned to Seward not only for counsel but for companionship. He spent more evenings at Seward's convivial home than with Mary Todd Lincoln at the White House. They regularly attended the theater together. They traveled together and joked together, even at each other's expense.

One anecdote tells of the two riding in a mule-drawn wagon while the driver cussed up a storm. Finally Lincoln, who seldom swore, asked, "My friend, are you by chance an Episcopalian? You sound just like Mr. Seward here."

Seward not only had a salty tongue, he was also chastised for rough manners, presumptuousness and being too familiar with women. All was forgiven, however, because of his quirky and generally likable personality. He drank and smoked; Lincoln did neither, but he enjoyed comic wit and insight, which Seward could supply. Likewise, Seward stood ready to laugh at Lincoln's jokes. Some members of the Cabinet were offended when the two took time at meetings to read newspaper humor columns.

The President, whom some modern psychiatrists have diagnosed as suffering from depression, may have needed laughter to get through the bleakness of the war. But the laughter was not frivolous, Seward said. "I never heard (Lincoln) make a pun. And (I) rarely heard him tell an anecdote unless it illustrated something."

Other historians find the friendship a bit lopsided. They hold that Seward's vanity kept him from giving Lincoln the camaraderie that Lincoln showed him. Similarly, they assert, he was incapable of returning the dedication of his wife.

But he was selflessly dedicated to his nation. In one tough trial he wrote to Frances that he had but one "simple line of action to pursue, that is to be faithful; faithful to the country and to its cause."

A new problem arose at sea. In 1862 the Confederacy obtained a warship from Britain, the *CSS Alabama*, and it was sinking American commercial ships left and right. Britain was preparing to sell the Confederacy state-of-the-art torpedo rams and France was likewise building warships for the South. Seward impressed on both countries that if they released the ships the United States would consider it an act of war and would, in fact, declare war against the countries that had provided the weapons.

That was a bluff. Both France and England knew America did not have the naval power to confront them while simultaneously blockading the South. But something had changed since Fort Sumter. Where the United States had been thought of as a remote and irrelevant peculiarity among the more-or-less civilized nations, it was now seen as a world power. And where Seward had been caricatured as an ignorant blowhard, easily dismissed, he was now seen as a serious statesman of the first order.

Europe considered its options and remained neutral.

1863 was the pivotal year in the war. In the West, General Ulysses Grant took control of the Mississippi River from New Orleans to St. Louis. In the East, Lee led a large army into Pennsylvania where it was confronted by a somewhat larger Union force near Gettysburg. At the end of three days of fighting more than 40,000 men were dead. Lee was in retreat and the tide of the war had permanently turned in favor of the Union.

The threat of European intervention was over. Seward took foreign diplomats on a "grand tour" of New York where they could see for themselves the prosperous farms, busy factories and flourishing cities.

In the fall of that year, the Russian fleet made goodwill stops in New York and San Francisco. It was a show of force, just in case Britain or France had any lingering thoughts about breaking the blockade.

The Russian officers were feted at the White House and at a spectacular dinner at Seward's house, a seven course meal served on imperial china from France and seven flights of wine capped with Havana cigars.

One aspect of the Russian visit that no one at the time noticed — not the press, not Seward's friends or his enemies — had to do with conversations about Russian America. With California now a state, the United States and Russia were near neighbors. Seward wanted Americans on the West Coast to have access to the resources of the North Pacific. Russia hinted that it might be willing to sell its claims.

Officially, that was off the record. The Russian Empire had been expanding since the 1500s and had never willingly relinquished a square foot of territory.

But in New Archangel, Governor Furuhjelm sensed a shift in policy. A team of officials traveled from St. Petersburg with orders to investigate every corner of the Russian-American Company's business. They pored over the books, inspected inventories and properties, asked questions about the treatment of the indigenous people.

Furuhjelm had been under the impression that he was doing a good job. Troubles with the Tlingit had ended after he predicted an eclipse and told the cowering Natives that he would take the sun away permanently if they didn't behave.

At least that was his version of the story. It was remembered somewhat differently in Sitka lore. Tlingits had gone to Russian universities and studied navigation and astronomy. They knew all about eclipses.

What Furuhjelm did that truly impressed Native Alaskans was that he traveled without an armed guard, sometimes with just an interpreter.

Furuhjelm nervously asked the inspectors if he'd done something wrong. Was the company mad at him?

"No, not the company," they replied. The books were in order, people seemed content, the place was making a profit on sales of ice and salt fish to San Francisco. "It's the Grand Duke Konstantin," the Tsar's brother, they said. "He can't stand the colony."

During Furuhjelm's term in New Archangel, Russia had established a river route from Central Asia to the Pacific. The Grand Duke was insisting that the Empire no longer needed North America, which might be a liability.

The Governor understood the realities. Hudson's Bay steamships were zipping in and out of his territory trading with the Chilkats to the north. Koh'klux had never accepted Russian authority and Furuhjelm knew better than to show up on his turf, armed or unarmed. Furuhjelm's tour of duty was due to end in 1864. He and Anna were already planning for their move with the "three small Americans" born to them in New Archangel. One, Annie Furuhjelm, would become a writer and publisher, a member of the Finnish parliament and a key proponent of the international women's suffrage movement. In the context of world history, she remains probably the most important person ever born in Sitka.

On November 18, 1863, Seward traveled with Lincoln to dedicate the cemetery at Gettysburg. They arrived at 6 p.m. and took rooms in neighboring houses. Lincoln had prepared remarks to deliver the following day. A crowd gathered and asked him to speak. He declined, so they went to where Seward was staying and he was only too happy to address those assembled.

At 11 p.m. Lincoln called on Seward. The two had a private meeting that lasted an hour or more. What they talked about has never been disclosed, but some scholars are of the opinion that Lincoln's short speech scrawled on the back of an envelope underwent fine tuning.

The next morning Lincoln and Seward toured the battlefield. Then they sat through a two hour speech by former Secretary of State Edward Everett. When it was over, Lincoln rose and said a few words beginning with "Four score and seven years ago" and concluding with the promise that "this nation, under God ... shall not perish from the earth."

No one has ever proved that Seward had any input into the Gettysburg Address, but it has a distinct echo of what Seward said to the crowd the night before: "This government of ours must be ... and will be immortal."

Nineteen: Endgame

JEFFERSON C. DAVIS
BV'T. GENL. U.S.A.

U.S. Army General Jefferson Columbus Davis, future commander of the Military District of Alaska, depicted in action during the Civil War. Photo from the Library of Congress.

General Grant took over command of the Union Army in the East at the end of 1863. For two years the Confederacy had fought their bigger, better armed enemy to a stalemate, helped by a succession of Northern generals who were too timid or too incompetent to use their advantage. With Grant, Lincoln looked for a change.

Seward chaperoned the new champion of the North around Washington, introducing him to key members of Congress and administration officials. Like Seward, Grant drank and constantly smoked cigars. Unlike Seward, Grant was not a negotiator. His nickname was

"Unconditional Surrender Grant." He held no romantic notions about combat and was relentless about getting the job done.

Seward and Lincoln hoped that between Vicksburg and Gettysburg the South would realize that it could not win and sue for peace. It must have been bitter medicine to hear Grant's frank appraisal of the situation. Yes, he could crush the enemy, but it would not be quick or easy. The foe was stubborn and ferocious. To restore the Union many more lives would need to be spent.

In their hearts, they knew he was right. Both the President and the Secretary of State maintained a tone of reconciliation, but from here on the fighting would be left to Stanton and Grant.

The spring campaign in Virginia was a slog through carnage. In the West the Yankees suffered a spectacular defeat at Shreveport. But throughout the North there was the sense that their side was now winning.

Seward used this time to push for immigration reforms he had wanted since he was Governor of New York. He saw another long-held dream born in 1863 as construction began on a transcontinental railroad with the goal of linking the American Empire from Atlantic to Pacific.

The job of communicating with foreign governments had been hampered by the fact that it took the mail weeks to go from America to Europe. Seward envied Stanton's ability to instantly receive reports and issue orders halfway across the country via telegraph. He repeatedly encouraged the development of a cable under the Atlantic, but early attempts to establish it had been trouble-plagued and short-lived. It seemed that the ingenuity of man would be no match for the mighty ocean.

So Seward looked for a different route. He lobbied Congress to support a line through Canada, down the Yukon River and across the Bering Strait to Asia. It would connect with the European network spreading eastward from Moscow.

In a communication to Congress, he asserted that the plan couldn't be harder than stringing the wire to California through hostile Indian territory. The Indian tribes along the American part of the route "have been so well subjected to the influences of society and government ... that no serious resistance from them need be apprehended," he said. "The inhabitants of Asiatic Russia (are) not savage, like the American natives. After centuries of internal war, they have now settled into a state of semi-civilization."

Seward's main business in 1864 was the reelection of Lincoln. The country was weary of the war and many blamed the President. In the wake of the Emancipation Proclamation, abolition was a hot-button issue. A number of politicians held grudges against Seward and thought the only way to remove him was to remove the President.

Salmon Chase began to position himself to dethrone his boss. George McClellan likewise prepared a campaign just as Confederates made yet another invasion of Union territory. Thurlow Weed, working closely with Seward to secure the party nomination for Lincoln, worried that the President might face defeat.

Seward saw reasons for optimism. Grant had stalled before Richmond, but the month of May brought two Union shows of force. Phil Sheridan ran a circle around Lee's army, destroying tracks and telegraph lines. And a 100,000 man force under William Sherman departed Tennessee to attack Atlanta, the economic hub of the Confederacy.

Sherman's march, without lines of support, remains breathtaking in both scope and audacity. Lincoln and Grant had reviewed his plan and approved it, giving him the pick of commanders to assist him. One of the men he picked was Jef Davis.

Sherman reached Atlanta in September and burned it to the ground. He then continued to the sea. As the Union Army swept past plantations they were joined by throngs of jubilant blacks. Their numbers grew until Sherman worried that they put his troops at risk. The invasion force was in no position to both fight the Rebels and feed a mob of people who knew they were now free, but weren't sure what that meant.

The Confederacy's best cavalry commander, General Joseph Wheeler, closed in on the rear flanks of Sherman's army as the Union troops crossed the defile at Ebenezer Creek. Like he had at Fort Moultrie, Davis stayed until the last minute before he ordered his soldiers across the bridge. Then, with the liberated slaves still on the other side, he had it blown up, leaving them for Wheeler to deal with.

Word of this incident reached Washington before Sherman reached Savannah in December. He had no sooner taken the city than a boat came ashore with none other than War Secretary Stanton himself. Stanton was steaming mad and insisted on putting Davis in chains. Sherman rejected the suggestion. He was only halfway done with his march and Davis was indispensable. They were trying to win a war, not run a charity.

Stanton was not placated, but Sherman was now a national hero and the War Secretary had to back down.

As Seward predicted, Lincoln handily won the election of 1864. The Democratic challenger, McClellan, proved to be as ineffective a campaigner as he was a general. The self-aggrandizing Chase resigned from the Cabinet shortly after Lincoln received the endorsement of the Republicans, temporarily known as the Union Party. To assuage his anti-slavery wing, Lincoln gave Chase the position of Chief Justice of the Supreme Court.

1865 began with Grant inching toward Richmond, sometimes sacrificing as many men in a week as Lee had in his entire army, and Sherman slicing gloriously through the Carolinas to join him. Talk in the Cabinet turned toward postwar policies.

Two issues were of top importance. First, under what conditions the rebellious states would be readmitted to the Union. Lincoln favored a lenient policy. If ten percent of eligible voters renounced the Confederacy, a state could hold elections that Washington would honor. States would retain all the prerogatives they had held before the war, except for slavery.

Seward approved this welcome-back approach, but many of the new class of congressmen were adamant that the South should be punished. The so-called radical Republicans blamed Seward's influence for making Lincoln go soft on the Rebels, although the President was plainly keeping to a position he had held throughout his presidency.

The slavery issue was the second concern. The Dred Scott decision was still the law of the land; the Constitution did not allow the federal government to outlaw slavery in individual states.

So the Constitution had to be amended. Here Seward, Lincoln and the radicals could all agree. The Senate, led by Charles Sumner, readily approved the Thirteenth Amendment prohibiting slavery in April of 1864. There was opposition, however, from members of the House of Representatives who felt slavery would be necessary for the South's economy and that freed blacks would not be able to take care of themselves without the plantation system. Other politicians wanted no new powers given to the national government and no dilution of state authority. And many members of Congress expected favors or bribes in exchange for their votes.

Seward became the lead lobbyist for the amendment, building a coalition across party lines and cajoling editors and journalists to write in its support. The measure would not pass the House until January

31, 1865, but barely, and only with the help of 15 Democrats.

As the anti-slavery amendment was being debated in the Senate, word came from Confederate officials that they wanted to discuss peace. Lincoln and Seward met the envoys under truce on board the paddlewheel steamer *River Queen* near Hampton, Virginia. The Confederacy was represented by its Vice President, Alexander Stevens, Senator Robert Hunter and Assistant Secretary of War John Campbell. Seward had been friends with all of them when they had held similarly high offices in the United States Congress and Supreme Court.

The conversation was cordial, even convivial, with Lincoln spinning his famous stories and Seward punctuating the conversation with his wit. But in the end there could be no compromise. The parties left sadly and the war resumed.

Seward began thinking about life after Washington. He planned to expand the house in Auburn. Frances was dismayed at the idea. It had been her only home since childhood and she grieved at any change. But her husband was deaf to her concerns.

On April 3, 1865, Grant took Richmond. Lincoln made a trip to the conquered Confederate capital where he was greeted as a second Moses by freed slaves. Seward would have met him there except for a fateful accident.

Twenty: Night of Blood

ATTEMPTED ASSASSINATION OF WM. H. SEWARD, SECRETARY OF STATE.

A newspaper illustration of Lewis Powell's attempt on Seward's life, part of the conspiracy that included the killing of Abraham Lincoln.
From the National Police Gazette.

On the afternoon of April 5 Seward was riding in an open carriage with Frederick, Fanny and her friend Mary Titus. The door swung open and, as the driver dismounted to secure it, the horses spooked and bolted. The driver, still holding the reins, was jerked off his feet. Frederick jumped out to assist, but fell. The carriage raced on without him.

Seward stood up and leaped over the side, apparently thinking he could help halt the team. Instead he fell headfirst, fracturing his right arm, smashing his nose and breaking his jaw on both sides.

Passers-by stopped the horses. They found Seward unconscious and carried him back to his house. Doctors told the family his injuries were life-threatening. Frederick, who had not been seriously hurt in his fall, sent word to his mother to come from Auburn as fast as she could.

One of Seward's first visitors was Stanton. The war chief stayed at his side like a nurse. Stanton "wiped his lips — spoke gently to him — and was like a woman in the sickroom," Fanny wrote. Seward was brought to tears by his colleague's concern.

Stanton wired news of the accident to Lincoln. The President rushed back to Washington and made a beeline to Seward's house. He stretched out on the bed next to the injured man and talked with him. "I think we are near the end at last," he said.

It was Stanton who brought Seward news that Lee had surrendered. The war was over. Seward brightened and made Stanton give him complete details.

The next day, however, he felt worse. Doctors gave him a sleeping potion that left him confused and babbling. They changed out the bandages and attached a large wire brace to his teeth, stretching across his neck and mouth. It held the jaw firmly in place, a cumbersome splint that Frances called "a constant source of irritation."

It may have saved his life.

At 10 p.m. on April 14, 1865, "The gas lights were turned low and all was quiet" in the Seward house, Frederick recalled. Fanny, who had been reading Tennyson's "Enoch Arden" out loud to Seward, sat next to his bed. An Army nurse, George Robinson, was also in the room.

The patient had enjoyed a good day. He had eaten some soft food for the first time since the accident and was resting as comfortably as he could with the miserable brace stuck to his mouth.

There was a commotion outside the door. Fanny cracked it open to ask for quiet and saw Frederick standing on the stairway a few steps above a very large stranger.

The stranger looked up and, with a curse, drew a gun, pointed it at Frederick and pulled the trigger. Nothing happened, so he used the gun to bash at Frederick's head. Fanny slammed the door, but the stranger pushed through, now holding a large Bowie knife. Robinson attempted to stop him, but was slashed and knocked down. Fanny, too, was pushed to the floor.

The stranger fell on Seward, holding him down, repeatedly stabbing at his face and neck. Seward struggled and rolled off the other side of the bed. Robinson continued to try to pull the stranger away, but the man resolutely came around the bed to continue his attack.

By now — a matter of seconds, really — Fanny's screams had alerted the household. Her oldest brother Augustus came in and, with Robinson's help, got the assailant out of the room. Augustus ducked into his room to grab a pistol, "inspiring the assassin with hasty impulse to retreat." The stranger stabbed a State Department messenger on the stairs and escaped into the night.

Seward's throat was cut on both sides, his right cheek nearly severed from his face. Robinson was wounded, Augustus had a serious cut on one hand and two slashes to the bone on his head. The messenger had been knifed in the spine.

Frederick had been struck so fiercely that the gun broke. His skull was fractured in two places. Surgeons ultimately removed eight pieces of bone from his brain.

Lying in a puddle of his own blood, Seward managed to mumble, "I'm not dead." Some say the brace deflected the knife at critical points.

If Seward's condition was serious, Frederick's was perilous. It took a fortnight for him to return to full consciousness and for weeks after that the family worried that the open gashes would start to fatally hemorrhage.

Throughout the next day, Seward remained mostly unconscious. But the day after, Easter Sunday, he asked to be carried to a window. From there he saw flags at half-mast.

"The President is dead," he said.

Not wanting to upset him, his attendant denied it. But Seward continued. "If he had been alive he would have been the first to call on me. But he has not been here ... and there's the flag at half-mast."

Frances had tried to tell him earlier about what had happened at Ford's Theatre, but he had not understood her. Now he knew the truth. He slumped in his bed, weeping.

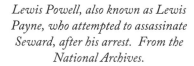
Lewis Powell, also known as Lewis Payne, who attempted to assassinate Seward, after his arrest. From the National Archives.

His would-be murderer, a former Confederate soldier named Lewis Powell, was in league with John Wilkes Booth. While Booth was at the theater killing Lincoln with a bullet to the head, Powell's assignment was to dispatch Seward, whom Booth saw as the machiavellian Mark Anthony to Lincoln's dictatorial Caesar. A third killer was supposed to murder Vice President Andrew Johnson, but lost his nerve.

Booth escaped to Virginia where he was tracked down and shot on April 26. Powell was arrested and subjected to a torturous trial that was inhumane even by the standards of 1865, forced to wear a suffocating padded hood 23 hours a day. The stifling headpiece caused such discomfort that he tried to kill himself by bashing his head against a wall. His jailers simply added more padding.

He was hanged on July 7 with three other similarly ill-treated conspirators.

Frances did not live to see justice. "This baptism of blood seems to have obliterated much of my previous existence," she wrote soon after the attack. "The wearing anxiety I feel about Mr. Seward and Frederick consumes my strength."

Her health had not been good for several years. The stress of the assassination attempt was too much. She died on June 21, 1865.

Twenty-one: After Lincoln

The execution of the Lincoln assassination conspirators.
Lewis Powell is second from the left. From the Library of Congress.

The recoveries of both William and Frederick Seward bordered on miraculous. By the middle of the summer Seward was back at his duties. While he was initially inclined to punish all of the Rebel leaders, he soon returned to Lincoln's point of view and began lobbying for pardons, particularly for the many Confederate officials who had been his friends prior to the war.

In November he wrote to his daughter that his home had become "the chief resort of the recently rebels." The following summer he entertained the elected congressional representatives from Tennessee. "I had a calf served up in many ways," he wrote to Fanny, "and they accepted it as returned prodigals."

There were rumblings that Congress would not seat representatives from states that had seceded.

Seward thought such restrictions unwise. But radical legislators were implacable.

At least he could savor one hard-won victory when the requisite number of states ratified the Thirteenth Amendment. It was nearly 20 years since he had declared, "Slavery can and must be abolished." On December 18, as Secretary of State, it fell to him to sign the certification making the anti-slavery amendment part of the Constitution. He put his name on the great parchment sheet with a deep sense of satisfaction.

His main job remained foreign policy. On July 29 he received the first dispatch announcing the success of the Trans-Atlantic cable. "I am … very much wondering how the Atlantic Telegraph may modify my business habits," he wrote to Fanny.

Slow overseas communications had been a serious obstacle throughout the war. Two and a half months after Lee's surrender on April 9, 1865, a Confederate warship, the *Shenandoah*, captured 21 Yankee whaling ships off the coast of Russian America, burning most of them. The Rebel captain would not receive certain news of the South's defeat until August.

The destruction of American-flagged merchant ships by the tiny Confederate Navy ruined many shippers. Seward blamed the British, who had built the ships and sold them to the Rebels. He demanded restitution.

Before the war, the British would have dismissed his objections. After dealing with William Seward for four years, however, there was a new sense of respect for the United States. When Seward suggested that both sides present their arguments to a neutral third party for adjudication, the Crown accepted his innovative proposal.

The *Alabama* Claims case, conducted in Geneva, Switzerland, set a new standard for international arbitration, a standard still used by nations who do not wish to settle their differences by war.

Another foreign policy success fell in his lap. France, seeing General Sheridan arrive at the Mexican border, announced it would withdraw its troops and encouraged Maximilian to come along with them. While the Civil War was on, Seward worried that if the United States sent troops to support the Juarez government, the South might suddenly declare peace with the Union in order to grab more slave-eligible territory.

With the war over and the slavery matter out of the way, Seward became a full-fledged advocate for expansion. Canada offered one possibility for new territory, particularly in the sparsely populated West. So did Cuba, Spain's last remaining New World possession of any size, and the Virgin Islands, owned by Denmark.

The Danes said they would sell the islands if the residents agreed. The capital of St. Thomas was of particular interest to Seward since lack of access to that port had been a hindrance to the United States Navy during the blockade of the South.

At the end of the year Seward and family members sailed through the Caribbean, visiting St. Thomas, the Dominican Republic, Haiti, Puerto Rico and Havana. It was the first time a sitting Secretary of State had traveled outside the country.

At each of the first three, he made overtures about purchasing strategic sites. All were receptive to one degree or another. But as Congress was considering acquiring the Virgin Islands a horrific hurricane wiped out St. Thomas and made Denmark's tropical paradise look like a bad investment.

In the meantime, the home front was deteriorating. Johnson wanted demilitarization of the South and a return to civilian rule as quickly as possible with few strings attached. Seward shared that opinion, in part because of his belief that persuasion was a better motivator than force, and also because such had been Lincoln's intention.

Lincoln might have smoothly persuaded the radicals into supporting his more lenient approach. But Johnson, a Union Democrat placed on the ticket in 1864 to attract votes in the border states, was no Lincoln. He had served as the military governor of Tennessee during the war and was accustomed to having his orders obeyed. He drank inappropriately, often before making important appearances, and grog seemed to bring out a nasty temper.

For the rest of his term, Seward repeatedly tried to get him to soften the language of his speeches, much as he advised Lincoln. Johnson not only ignored the advice, he rewrote his statements to make them even more inflammatory.

A bill to extend the Freedmen's Bureau, a temporary agency set up by Lincoln to assist the formerly enslaved transition to freedom, passed Congress with hardly a dissenting vote in February of 1866. Johnson determined to veto it. Seward urged him to sympathize with the intent of the bill's authors but frame his veto in terms of objections to details that could be addressed, probably willingly, by lawmakers who did not feel insulted.

Instead Johnson lambasted the legislators. An override of the veto failed by just a few votes, which Johnson took as a great victory. He used the occasion to ridicule not only the radicals in general, but their powerful leaders, Congressman Thaddeus Stevens and Senator Sumner, both friends of Seward.

In March a bill protecting the civil rights of blacks was passed. It stated that all persons born in the United States — except Indians — were citizens and entitled to the same rights and privileges. Johnson again vetoed it with caustic language. This time the veto was handily overridden.

The fracture between the President and Congress had become permanent and was widening. In advance of the congressional elections of 1866 Johnson made a barnstorming trip of the country with Seward and Grant. The "Swing Around the Circle" tour began well enough, but was met by hecklers in Ohio and Missouri. Johnson's improvised retorts amounted to hot-headed name-calling. In one rant he blamed the white-on-black violence that had erupted in many parts of the South on the radicals in Congress.

These remarks were carried in the Northern press and read with alarm. No-nonsense Grant left the tour in disgust. Stoeckl, the Russian ambassador, saw the trials on Seward's face. He described the Secretary as "aged and disfigured."

A week before the election, Seward experienced the most painful event in his life. His daughter Fanny, who suffered from tuberculosis, died on October 29 at the age of 21. She had been the apple of his eye. Her diaries and letters reveal a savvy observer with a genuine talent for writing. Even in a family where all the children were devoted to their father, she was especially close. She never expressed a desire for a husband, but hoped she would be able to achieve important work as a "useful unmarried woman."

After her death, Seward carefully collected all of her books and placed them in a special glass cabinet, still on view at the Seward House Museum in Auburn. They include the novels of Walter Scott, the plays of Molière and a Victorian curiosity titled "Leila, or, The Island" — the tale of a plucky girl marooned with her resourceful father.

The fall elections were a disaster for Seward, and perhaps for the country. He had pleaded with the voters to send moderates to Washington. Instead the radicals swept into power with veto-proof majorities in both houses of Congress.

The new majority wasted little time in seeing that Union soldiers continued to occupy the defeated states and impose congressional mandates on local populations. In Kentucky, which had not been part of the Confederacy but had number of Southern sympathizers, Jef Davis was named military commander.

Kentucky's Union and Confederate supporters alike opposed Davis' appointment. But his strict enforcement of regulations soon won their respect. He made it a point to protect and aid the freedmen. He countermanded laws that made the testimony of a black man inadmissible in Kentucky courts. He handily suppressed the cells of whites bent on re-suppressing blacks. He took pride in establishing a number of schools for freed slaves and their children and built a hospital for them.

An inspector sent to Kentucky wrote that Davis "settled the difficulties between the Negroes and white men with satisfaction to both and punished the lawless with such promptitude that even the bloody and much-feared 'regulators' were obliged, where he could reach their haunts, to suspend their base work of terrorism."

Duty was everything to Davis. If the Army wanted him to be an administrator, then he'd be the best administrator he could be. But he yearned for the opportunity to rejoin his old comrades-in-arms, now assigned to western posts where clashes with Indians had turned into a real war.

He eagerly awaited a transfer.

Twenty-two: A Deal is Made

Johnson's Democrats had no power in Congress in 1867. The radical Republicans quickly passed laws aimed at keeping the President from interfering with their plans for reconstructing the South, granting freedmen the right to vote and protecting them from mob violence. Johnson swore to veto all of them, even though the Republicans had plenty of votes to override him.

Seward was in sympathy with the purpose, if not the mechanism, of most of the reconstruction laws. But when Congress passed the Tenure of Office Act in early March, prohibiting Johnson from dismissing or appointing members of his own Cabinet, it was a step too far. Seward, with the rest of the cabinet, supported Johnson's veto of this bill. When it was duly overridden, he argued that it was still unconstitutional, a violation of the separation of powers, the prelude to a dictatorship of the legislative branch.

Washington politics, however, were not the only thing on his mind. Throughout the month of February of 1867, he had been in secret back-and-forth negotiations with Stoeckl regarding the purchase of Russian America. This time, it seemed, the Russians were serious.

Why would Tsar Alexander II wish to be first Russian monarch to hand over a chunk of the Empire? Historians give different reasons, but it cannot be overlooked that the Tsar was planning a new war against Turkey — and he hadn't yet paid off the debts of the Crimean War. While his main adversaries in that war, England and France, seemed less than eager to re-engage, there was always a possibility that Alexander would find himself facing the British Navy and the French Army. If that happened, his enemies would find New Archangel (Sitka) and Kodiak easy pickings.

Better to sell the colony, the Tsar's advisors said, rather than wait for someone to take it.

The new Atlantic telegraph cable meant trans-oceanic discussions took hours, not months or years. By the end of March, Seward and Stoeckl had negotiated a price of $7 million. Johnson and the Cabinet were on board.

One of the few members of Congress in the loop was Senator Sumner, Chairman of the Senate Foreign Relations Committee. As much as he hated Johnson and had come to distrust Seward, he kept the secret under wraps. When rumors circulated, it was easy to dismiss them. Sure, the Russians were talking, but they'd never followed through before. Why would they follow through this time?

Even Seward couldn't be sure. That's one reason why he abruptly abandoned his game of whist when Stoeckl showed up at his house after dark on March 29, 1867.

Frederick was dispatched to inform Sumner, then joined his father at the State Department. Copies of the treaty in English and French, the diplomatic language of Russia, were prepared and carefully compared. At dawn the finished paperwork was presented to Johnson for his approval. Seward then headed for the Senate, which was due to adjourn that day.

"While the Senate was about considering its favorite theme of administrative delinquency," Frederick writes, "the Sergeant-at-Arms announced, 'A message from the President of the United States.' Glances were significantly exchanged between Senators, with the muttered remark, 'Another veto!'"

The chamber was startled to hear Seward blurt out, "A treaty for the cession of Russian-America!"

Right on cue, Sumner rose in support of a speedy ratification. The Senate adjourned with the understanding that they would reconvene in a special session to consider the matter.

One Senator muttered, "I thought we were going to have another hack at Andy Johnson today, but it looks now as if we're going to vote for the biggest and most unheard-of thing the administration has done yet."

When the Senate reconvened Sumner spoke for three hours, stressing the resources of the territory, its strategic benefit to the country, and proposing the official name: Alaska. The treaty passed by a vote of 37 to 2.

Having been ratified by the Senate, the treaty was now the law of the land. The House was obligated to approve the funds to pay for it, $7.2 million being the final tab. However, they bided their time and didn't come up with the money until the following year. In the meantime Stoeckl anxiously made some strategic bribes and Seward put on a charm offensive. On the day of the House vote, July 14, 1868, he passed out invitations to a big party celebrating the new American possession — a party that everyone who was anyone wanted to go to.

But as tensions between the administration and legislature grew worse, the bribes could not escape investigation. Under oath, Seward calmly asserted that he knew nothing about any misuse of funds.

Whether he was lying was a moot point. Many House leaders had put their hands in the cookie jar, even the "incorruptible" Thaddeus Stevens. And most Americans were delighted with the purchase, particularly Americans on the West Coast.

The story that Seward was widely ridiculed for buying an "icebox" is a myth, though it remains current, even in Alaska. In Anchorage, 150 years after the purchase, there's a popular restaurant named "Seward's Folly."

Bret Harte gives a more accurate reflection of the mood of the time in his poem "An Arctic Vision," published in June of 1867. He extols the fur, cod and whaling, and hints at the possibility of gold in a tone both patriotic and humorous. "All ye icebergs make salaam — You belong to Uncle Sam!"

The diplomatic triumph of Alaska was accompanied by progress on several other fronts. Treaties were negotiated with Asian nations, including China and Japan. Rights of American citizens in foreign countries were established in Europe. It looked like British Columbia, with few people and large debts, might petition to join the United States.

The Mexico affair, on the other hand, took an unpleasant turn. The French Army departed even earlier than promised, but Maximilian refused to abandon his throne. He was captured and, despite the pleas of governments around the world, including the United States, executed on June 19, 1867.

Twenty-three: A Rough Transition

U.S. Army General Jefferson Columbus Davis, commander of the Military District of Alaska, hosted Seward's visit to Sitka and arranged for his meeting with Tlingit clan leader Koh'klux in Klukwan. Photo from the Library of Congress.

The summer went better for Jef Davis than for Maximilian. His transfer had finally arrived. He hastened to San Francisco to await orders.

He expected to be sent back to his old command. Instead the orders read, "You have been appointed Commander of the Military District of Alaska."

Davis may have wondered if this was his punishment for shooting Bull Nelson.

On October 9, 1867, Davis, his wife and 250 soldiers arrived in New Archangel, henceforth known as Sitka. There they awaited the

American and Russian officials who would oversee the official transfer of the colony. Those officials arrived on the morning of October 18 and, by 3:30 that afternoon, soldiers, officers, Russian and American civilians and high-ranking Tlingits were at the Governor's residence to witness the event.

General Lowell Rousseau, leading the American delegation, described Sitka as "quiet, orderly and law abiding," with a thousand or more Indians, 500 Russians, pigs, sheep and cows that gave "excellent milk."

"(The scenery is) as grand and beautiful as there is in the world," he wrote. "There is nothing like it on this continent."

The transfer took place on a bright and beautiful day. As the Russian flag was being lowered, it tangled in the ropes and got stuck halfway down. A makeshift boatswain's chair was rigged and a Russian soldier was drawn up. He detached the flag but then dropped it onto the bayonets of the Russian honor guard. There were cheers from the Americans.

"This was not part of the program," Rousseau wrote, "and in some respects I regretted that it occurred."

More miscues followed. The treaty allowed Russian Americans to leave or stay as U.S. citizens, but it made no provision for the many who lived in quarters provided by the Russian-American Company. The company's buildings — like the icebergs in Harte's poem — now belonged to Uncle Sam. Davis evicted the civilian residents to make room for his soldiers, the largest professional armed force that had ever landed in Alaska.

A cadre of opportunistic Americans, including one William Dodge, a passing acquaintance of Seward's, tried to grab power, declaring themselves the elected officers of Sitka. Their "city council" excluded creole and Indian residents. Some of the newcomers arranged a kangaroo court in which they presumed to sue the departing Russian governor. The San Francisco firm of Hutchinson, Kohl and Co., run by Dodge's brother-in-law, acquired the remaining Russian-American stock and proceeded to sell goods and buy furs with the leverage of a full monopoly.

The complaints of all came to Davis. Since Congress had not provided for any form of civilian government, keeping order fell to the military.

It was not an easy job. Rather than put up with the affronts of Dodge and his friends, most disgusted Russian Alaskans and many creoles left for the motherland. The rapacious whites quarreled with each other and bribed soldiers and port officials.

The Hudson's Bay Company continued to run through what were now American waters, getting black market furs from Natives, often trading guns and alcohol. More troubling, British agents spread rumors that Americans were not to be trusted.

The Indians had their own laws, which Russia had largely ignored. Various degrees of slave-holding were practiced by both Russians and Natives of Russian America even after Tsar Alexander abolished it in Russia by emancipating the serfs in 1861.

Davis didn't attempt to change that, but he did intercede to stop the custom of killing slaves at certain ceremonies. He was less effective in ending the practice of blood retribution, by which a violent death or affront was answered by killing a member of the offending clan.

Dodge and Davis quickly butted heads. The would-be boomer slipped reports to newspapers suggesting that Davis was profiting from liquor sales to Indians and otherwise abusing his position.

The Alaska Herald, published in English and Russian in San Francisco, repeated some of these charges. "General Davis at Sitka can be very easily bribed for a box of cigars and case of wine," wrote editor Agapius Honcharenko. "Very cheap, indeed!"

Honcharenko, whose main advertiser was a Hutchinson competitor, directed most of his fire at the monopoly and at Dodge. He accused Dodge of enabling smuggling, driving Russians out of Alaska and philandering.

"We have good reason for bestowing on him the title of Abdul Pasha," he wrote. "Brigham Young Dodge would not be inappropriate."

As he advocated for the dwindling Russian population, so Honcharenko defended the Natives, whom he described as "morally superior to the whites around them."

"We assert and believe that natives of Alaska are natives of Russian America and have more right to have privileges granted to them than emigrants from Europe," he wrote. Tlingits and Aleuts had hoped for friendly relations with the newcomers, but soon discovered that "the white men have no sympathies with them and declined to meet their advances in a friendly spirit."

Davis believed that Alaska's Natives needed to be "governed with a firm hand and a watchful eye." He also saw that "many of them understand justice and impartiality and appreciate it."

Eadweard Muybridge, who took photographs of Alaska under U.S. government contract in 1868, observed that "the Indians are well advanced in the industrial arts … polished and educated."

Even Dodge spoke well of the Tlingits. "They are of a very superior intelligence," he said, noting their houses were "neatly built and far more substantial and pretentious than the log houses usually constructed by our manly backwoodsmen."

According to Tlingit historian Herbert Hope, the Sitka tribe was nervous at the presence of so many soldiers. But they came to respect Davis' impartiality. When a Tlingit and a Russian found themselves arrested for drunken misbehavior and placed in a cell with a soldier, jailed for the same offense, the story was widely repeated in the Tlingit community.

When soldiers looted the Orthodox Church, taking jeweled and golden sacred objects, Davis had the culprits drummed out of the service in an impressive public humiliation and shipped off with orders never to return.

Despite such actions, the soldiers, far from home and bored to the point of suicide, were a bigger problem for Davis than Dodge or the Tlingits. They did things he couldn't fathom. Some of the bluecoats who had just fought to end black slavery were buying Indian children to be their own personal slaves.

It did not improve when the Army command, counting on Davis' reputation as a disciplinarian, sent their most dangerous military prisoners to Sitka to provide forced labor.

Twenty-four: Impeachment

Andrew Johnson, who became president after the assassination of Abraham Lincoln.
Seward arranged Johnson's defense during his impeachment trial in 1868.
From the Library of Congress.

In 1868 Seward faced a crisis that, to his mind, was nearly as much a threat to the American Republic as secession had been in 1861.

Congress and the President were irreconcilably alienated. Members of Johnson's own Cabinet — Lincoln's Cabinet — opposed him. Chief among them was Secretary of War Stanton. In August of 1867 Johnson demanded his resignation. Stanton refused. Johnson suspended him and appointed Grant as the acting Secretary of War.

Stanton barricaded himself in the War Department and refused to leave.

Fortunately, America was not at war. But the stand-off put Seward in a difficult position. Johnson's behavior in office had created a level of toxic animosity between the branches of government that has never been seen since. It undermined Seward's attempts to expand the United States' empire. It caused old friends to turn against him, Sumner, Stevens and now Stanton.

He offered his own resignation, but Johnson refused to accept it. Worries about whom Johnson might nominate to replace him and how that replacement might jeopardize the work of the State Department convinced Seward to stay on.

In January of 1868 Grant, realizing he was being used, left his "acting" post and Johnson made formal the dismissal of Stanton.

The following month the House voted to impeach Johnson on a list of catch-all charges that included violating the Tenure of Office Act.

Many radicals blamed Seward for Johnson's actions. His longtime ally Thurlow Weed said he'd become the most hated man in America. Overtures were made to pull him away from the President. Renounce Johnson and you'll be a hero, he was told.

"I'll see you damned first," was his reply

Why did Seward choose to be branded as a turncoat rather than side with his own party? It may have stemmed from his study of what happened to democracies in Central and South America when one branch of government abrogated constitutions. If Congress could dismiss a chief executive without serious cause, he felt, the Republic of Washington, Adams, Jefferson and Lincoln would soon be reduced to a brawl, partisans devouring one another. America would become a series of shaky usurpations with power shifting between dictatorial oligarchies and tyrants.

The dismissal of Stanton was a bad decision, he thought. But it did not threaten the existence of the nation the way impeachment might under these circumstances.

Seward took the lead in preparing Johnson's defense. Working with Democrats and the few moderate Republicans still speaking to him, he obtained a top defense team and raised funds to cover their costs. He turned to the most powerful lobbyist in Washington, Cornelius Wendell, a man who knew the minds — and the price — of every member of Congress better than they knew themselves.

The solution was clear, Wendell said: Buy the votes of Senators.

The cost: a quarter of a million dollars. Seward raised the money. Wendell got it to the right people.

The House having voted to impeach Johnson in February, it now fell to the Senate to try the President in accord with Article II of the Constitution. The trial began on March 30, 1868, and lasted for six weeks. A two-thirds majority would be needed to oust Johnson from office. On May 16 the vote was called. The tally was 35-19. Johnson escaped impeachment by one vote.

In the following weeks the House tried to take additional actions, but they too fell short. Both sides were exhausted. Johnson's term was coming to an end. War hero Grant would be the next President. There was no point in expending any more effort.

Seward strove to wind up various matters still on his desk — like the matter of actually paying Tsar Alexander II the money due for Russian America.

Twenty-five: Trouble in Sitka

Photography pioneer Eadweard Muybridge took the first known photos of Alaska in 1868. This uniquely unposed scene shows Tlingit Indians in Sitka or Wrangell relaxing near the water. Some are traditionally clothed while others, perhaps mixed-race "creole" relatives, appear to be wearing European-style clothes. From the Library of Congress.

The check that bought Alaska was issued on August 1, 1868, more than nine months after Jef Davis had taken command of the military district.

A month or two after Stoeckl cashed the check, Koh'klux arrived in Sitka with a contingent of 50 Chilkats. Davis knew of his reputation as "the most powerful and vindictive chief on this coast" and found him "a very haughty and imperious man."

Koh'klux's visit included negotiations in a long-running dispute over retribution for Chilkats who had been killed by Sitka people some years before. The chiefs of other villages, including Wrangell and Kake, were also in town.

A curfew was enforced on the Indian village below the Governor's mansion from 7 a.m. to 7 p.m. Davis had a sentry posted at the village gate. On New Year's Day of 1869 Koh'klux returned to the village after curfew. When the sentry challenged him, he grabbed the man's gun and walked off with it. Koh'klux was not afraid to fight, but he knew that sometimes humiliation was as good as battle, and a lot more fun.

Davis saw nothing to joke about. He sent a contingent of soldiers to arrest the chief. They were fired upon, most likely by the Chilkats, and returned fire, killing at least one Indian — a bystander from Kake. The village went into uproar. The soldiers retreated to their fort. Throughout the night the white population of Sitka braced for an attack.

In the morning Davis summoned the Sitka leaders and showed them his cannons aimed at the village. They protested that they had nothing to do with the altercation. Then give me Koh'klux, Davis said. To do so would mean war with the Chilkats, they replied, and they didn't want that any more than they wanted a war with the U.S. Army. They would stay neutral, raising white flags over their houses. But they would not surrender the clan chief of Klukwan.

As the day wore on Davis seemed on the verge of firing. He had a bead on the place where he thought Koh'klux was staying. But he hesitated several times. A sergeant heard him say, "My God, I don't want to destroy so many innocent people for one man."

His interpreter was too terrified to return to the village. So Davis decided to go in himself. As his men looked on in dread, he walked out the gate, down the hill and into the a crowd of several hundred equally astonished Indians. He walked alone to the house where Koh'klux was staying and placed him under arrest.

"It was the most wonderful thing I ever saw, and there ain't another man but General Davis would do it," the sergeant recalled.

Koh'klux was surely as flabbergasted as everyone else at Davis' audacity. But he submitted when he saw he could expect no help from the Sitka people. The anger they felt toward the Chilkats was greater than their distrust of the Americans.

That was not the end of the matter. In the wake of the excitement Davis ordered all Indians to stay in town until he decided they could travel. A group from Kake nonetheless tried to paddle out of the harbor at night. They were fired on and captured. One was wounded. Davis let the other eight go.

On their way home the Kake men came across two white men and killed them, blood retribution for the man killed in the clash in Sitka.

Davis now went to war in earnest. He took the Navy cutter *Saginaw* to Kake. The villagers, alerted to the coming attack, fled. Finding the place deserted, Davis' soldiers burned houses and canoes. The Kake people spent the rest of the winter hungry and cold, hiding in the woods or falling on the kindness of neighboring villages.

Modern historians are of the opinion that Davis overreacted. *The Alaska Herald* held that opinion, blaming Davis for the whole affair. So did the *Herald's* arch-enemy, William Dodge.

Complaints reached his commanders, who had their hands full fighting bloody battles with Paiute, Sioux, Modoc and other tribes in the West. They approved of his actions.

While Koh'klux was still in jail, George Davidson, an astronomer with the United States Coast Survey, arrived with an unusual request of Davis. A full eclipse of the sun was due to take place on August 7. Klukwan, the main settlement of the feared Chilkats, would provide an ideal viewing spot. Did the General think it was safe to go there?

Davis met with his prisoner and offered his freedom if he would promise that Davidson and his party would not be molested when they came to Klukwan. Koh'klux assured him that they would be treated as honored guests.

A Chilkat chief's promise was his very breath.

Twenty-six: To Alaska

William Seward in 1870 during his trip around the world. His age and injuries clearly show on his face in this photo taken in China. From the collection of the Seward House Museum, Auburn NY.

Koh'klux returned to Klukwan while Andrew Johnson was preparing to depart Washington, a humiliated and failed leader, the first in a string of mediocrities who would succeed him as President for the next 16 years. Seward, also under a cloud, was leaving with him.

He had earned many enemies during his tenure, but he found he had also won much respect. People he barely knew or perhaps didn't know at all showered him with gifts. One Abram Wakeman sent "a small package of seegers which I beg you to accept." Sabras Iturbide, who described himself as a "poor and very humble Mexican, in his transports of satisfaction at the abolition of slavery in the United States" sent him an ink stand. Seward returned to Auburn with so much wine that he joked his cellar would be stocked for life.

But the house in Auburn seemed lonely. His wife and daughters were buried at Fort Hill Cemetery. Politics held no future for him. He could feel his age. Paralysis began to affect his right arm, the arm broken in the carriage accident.

During his years in office, he had dreamed of a railroad that connected America from east to west. He had persistently promoted that idea, even during the heat of the Civil War. Now, as he began retirement, he saw that dream fulfilled. In May of 1869 the transcontinental railroad was completed. A ribbon of steel ran across the map of America from ocean to ocean. And at the top of that map was Alaska.

It was time to take a trip.

Seward had invitations to visit San Francisco, with a special railcar on the just-completed railroad and free transport of packages courtesy of Wells Fargo. The Treasury Department put its revenue cutters at his disposal and General Sherman instructed all Army officers on the Pacific Coast to extend any services Seward might require "promptly and civilly." His "goofy" son William, who had become a very successful banker, arranged for him to draw on $10,000 in funds as needed.

In early June, he went to the graves of Frances, Cornelia and Fanny. He spent several minutes in silent reflection, then turned his face toward the Pacific. He boarded the train with his son Frederick and Frederick's wife Anna.

On paper the trip to California could have taken less than a week. But Seward was anxious to see and savor as much as he could of the people and natural marvels of the country. The journey lasted almost a month.

The ribbon of steel was not quite complete. The travelers had to cross the Missouri River by boat. They were held up in Nebraska by Indian troubles on the route ahead, but then proceeded to Cheyenne without incident. A stagecoach ride was arranged for a side trip to Denver, which was not yet connected to the railroad. Then they crossed the Continental Divide and made another side trip to Salt Lake City.

Seward was greeted there by Mormon leader Brigham Young, who asked about the home of one Squire Brown in Auburn. Surprised to hear the reference to his home town, Seward said he had once owned the property and lived in it. "I worked on that house as a journeyman carpenter when they were building it," Young said.

The Sewards were met by officials and businessmen from San Francisco and made the final leg of the journey by riverboat. The reception at midnight was tumultuous, with military parades, gun salutes, fireworks and throngs of exuberant people. Tired as he was, Seward made a well-received speech from the balcony of the Occidental Hotel, his headquarters during the stay.

The hotel filled with visitors each day. Gifts of California fruit and wine arrived. Every important group in town, from bankers to the Chinese American society met with him. He was the guest of honor at a constant succession of banquets and galas. When he took to the streets in a carriage, crowds followed him cheering and applauding.

"He received more than royal welcome," Frederick wrote, "the welcome of a free people to the greatest living representative of republican institutions. Never have I seen him in a finer flow of spirits, more alive to the innocent enjoyments of the present ... more hopeful of the grandeur of the future."

Frederick implies that the side trip to Alaska came on a whim after Seward reached California. More likely it was on his mind before he left Auburn. Shortly after he arrived in San Francisco, Admiral Thomas Craven, Commander of the Pacific Fleet, such as it was, told Seward his ships were out of service for repairs and he would be unable to spare the single available vessel for an excursion to Sitka.

The moguls of California stepped up. "We will be happy to place one of our steamers at the disposal of yourself... for the voyage to Alaska," wrote William Norton, Treasurer of the North Pacific Transportation Co.

On July 13, 1869, accompanied by several of the leading citizens of San Francisco, Seward departed on the *Active*, a luxurious steamship that Frederick compared to "a royal yacht." After a brief shore excursion at Port Orford, Oregon, the vessel headed to Victoria, British Columbia, arriving there on July 20.

While the *Active* proceeded to Nanaimo for re-coaling, Seward's party took a second ship to Puget Sound, stopping in Port Townsend, Seattle, Olympia and other ports.

As the voyage resumed, the *Active* became lost in the myriad islands and channels of the Inside Passage. While the captain squinted at unfamiliar landmarks, not knowing which way to go, a canoe with four Indians paddled up.

The leader offered to show a way to the passage north and was brought on board. The suspicious captain held a gun on him and indicated the guide would be shot if the ship ran aground, to which the Indian "grunted a ready assent." The other three men remained in the canoe, which was towed behind the steamer.

The guide knew the way. Once the ship had navigated through the maze he was given a large stack of silver 50-cent coins, "sitkum dollars," the standard unit of trade in the region. But Seward thought the three in the canoe also deserved something. The captain suggested that clothing was always welcome, whereupon Seward hurried below and returned with a cravat, a frock coat and a pair of pants that were passed to the men.

An Alaskan finds it curious that biographies of Seward make little mention of Native Americans except as proverbs or in the context of conflicts. This may say more about modern America than the country in 1869.

Seward must have known some Indians in his youth. They were a significant part of the New York population at the start of the 19th century. The Indian Removal policy that encouraged or forced tribes to relocate west of the Mississippi did not come about until the administration of John Quincy Adams. Seward was 27 and already involved in politics when the Buffalo Creek Treaty settled land claims with New York Indian nations. (Settled in theory; legal arguments about whether the terms have been fulfilled continue as of this writing, almost two centuries later.)

There were times when he expressed what sounds like sympathy. In 1831 he was outraged by the story of an educated and prosperous Mohican, "exemplary as a man, a citizen and a Christian, but whose death was hastened by the seduction of his two daughters by white men."

"What sin is there that white men have not committed against this simple race?" he wrote.

Then there was the imagined Indian who produced his rhetorical epitaph, "He was faithful," at the conclusion of the William Freeman trial.

But such passing remarks treat Native Americans as allegories or nostalgia, not as people who deserved advocacy and protection — the way he spoke of Irish, blacks and Chinese.

Whether as Governor, Senator or Secretary of State, Seward had little or no official business dealing with Indian affairs. Still, it is odd that little, if anything, is written about what this champion of immigrants, ally of escaping slaves, defender of the defenseless thought of the use of force by the country he loved against the original inhabitants.

The episode in the Inside Passage seems to be the first recorded personal encounter between Seward and any indigenous American. That was about to change.

Twenty-seven: Parlay at Klukwan

At Fort Simpson, Canada, on the coast of British Columbia (now called Port Simpson or Lax-Kw'alaami), Seward purchased several pieces of Haida art and was welcomed by the local matriarchal leader, "the Queen of the Haidas." The visitors were given beaver skins and entertained with songs and dances that Frederick critiques as being "entirely modest and not ungraceful." Seward reciprocated with more sitkum dollars. As he departed his hostess showered him with eagle down, a gesture of blessing and good will.

The *Active* arrived at Sitka on July 30, 1869. Seward visited Dodge, attended services at the Orthodox Cathedral with about 300 Russians and Indians, and then attended services at the Lutheran Church, the only Protestant Church allowed by the Russians.

He toured several enterprises of the area, a brewery, fish saltery, fur warehouse and a brand new sawmill. Davis prepared a banquet for him at which the Russian bishop, "a venerable, kindly prelate," and Tlingit leaders were present.

He took a walk through the Indian part of town, the same area that General Davis had risked his life to enter a few months earlier. Frederick found the Tlingits "a peaceable, good-natured race, very unlike the savages of the Atlantic States. They were not predatory and warlike but, in many respects, industrious and ingenious."

Seward went shopping and bought a number of Indian arts and crafts. He was fascinated by the totem poles seen everywhere in town. He likened their "fantastic savagery" to heraldic devices proudly displayed by Europeans.

Davis told Seward of Davidson's eclipse project in Klukwan and asked if he would like to join the expedition. Seward was hungry to see more, exactly as Davis had anticipated. He'd already sent word to Koh'klux that the "Great Tyee" — the chief who had bought the territory — was coming to visit.

Davis and his staff boarded the *Active* for the trip north. So did several members of the Sitka tribe, whose antipathy toward the Chilkats had only deepened after the mayhem of New Year's Day.

The voyage meandered throughout the "panhandle" of Alaska, to Mount St. Elias and the Lynn Canal. The weather turned rainy but Seward donned a slicker and stood on deck for glimpses of mountains and glaciers.

The party was met at the mouth of the Chilkat River by several canoes from Klukwan and escorted upriver to Koh'klux's great village. They were welcomed by the chief, who took the scars on Seward's face as the sign of a brave man.

Individual lodges were prepared for Seward, Davis and Davidson where they "passed a comfortable night in bear-skins and army blankets." It was the only time during his trip to Alaska that Seward spent a night on land.

The eclipse took place on August 7, 1869. Though the day started with typical Southeast Alaska rain and clouds, the skies cleared just before the event. Frederick's version speaks of the "visible anxiety" of the Tlingits as the sun was blocked out and a "weird, unusual light, which was neither night nor day," settled in. On board the *Active* some followed the progress looking through smoked glass or at reflections. The more devout Orthodox knelt and said the Lord's Prayer.

Frederick may have misread curiosity as anxiety. The Chilkats had seen the kind of high-tech instruments used by the scientific party — sextants, telescopes, chronometers. But to see so many in one place was unusual. The methodical execution of mathematical directions and assiduous note-taking by a man who wasn't even looking at the phenomenon must have resembled some kind of peculiar religious liturgy.

When the eclipse was over and bright light filled the blue sky, a mood of relief, satisfaction and "general cheerfulness" pervaded the assembly.

The shore party was about to return to the *Active* when Koh'klux summoned them to his clan house. The whites were ushered into a large building with a plain exterior of hand-hewn planks. Frederick describes hundreds of men and women standing "in grave, passive rows, all around the sides" of the interior. He does not mention gifts or dancing. This meeting was not an entertainment.

It may have crossed Davis' mind that he was in a potentially dangerous spot, surrounded by hundreds of Chilkat warriors, with only a small group of soldiers, most on board the *Active*, which was not a warship.

Within the traditional clan house a magnificent wood screen ran floor to ceiling along one side. Framing the middle of the room were four spectacular house posts, attributed to Kadjisdu.axtc, a sculptor of incomparable skill. Around 1800 he traveled from the southern part of the Tlingit realm to create art that would celebrate the fabulous wealth of the Chilkats in such a way as to leave no doubt in the minds of any who beheld it.

Gold Rush era photos of the "Big House of Koh'klux" hint at the glory of Kadjisdu.axtc's masterpieces, which are still magnificently displayed at the Jilkaat Kwaan Heritage Center in Klukwan.

This was the Parthenon, the Sistine Chapel of Alaska. Even Seward, who once scoffed that an hour in the Louvre was sufficient to make him an expert on art, must have found himself comparing what he saw to the monuments of Pharaohs and Caesars.

But Koh'klux's world was not a book or a lecture. It was real and present. And he, William Seward, had made it part of his own country, the youngest nation in the world meeting the magnificence of heroic antiquity in the chamber where he now stood.

If there was one moment in his life when Seward felt genuine humility, this was it.

The guests sat in the center as Koh'klux explained why he had brought them here. Sitka Indians had killed three Chilkats. What was the Great Tyee going to do about it?

Seward was caught off guard by the blunt demand. But he instantly grasped the situation. Koh'klux was in something of the same situation Seward had faced with the *Trent* crisis. A wrong had been done, but the cost of justice was disproportionate to the principle. On the other hand, failing to pursue justice would bring shame and possibly fracture the community. What action would both satisfy honor and restore cordial relations between the parties?

The game of whist is played with partners. One must form an educated guess about what his opponents have, how the other player's cards will affect his hand and, most important, how well he can trust his partner to make a smart play. Koh'klux would have been good at it.

A series of questions and answers followed. The killings had occurred when Russia owned Alaska, he was told, but the Tsar had not given satisfaction.

"Perhaps he was too poor. We know he was poor, because he had to sell his land to the Great Tyee. But now the Great Tyee himself is here," Koh'klux pointedly repeated, "and we want to know what he is going to do about it."

What would you have me do? Seward responded.

"A life for a life is the Indian law, and always has been," Koh'klux replied. And since the murdered Chilkats had been members of the chief's family, each of their lives was worth the lives of three commoners. The Chilkats wanted Seward's consent to kill nine Sitka people.

No killing would be allowed, Seward answered immediately. Don't even consider it. But, he added, "Is there any other form of reparation that you think might be made?"

Frederick saw the faces of the hosts light up as they heard Seward's words translated. "It began to look like business."

The Chilkats said they would accept four blankets for each of the Sitka people they might have killed. "Nine times four blankets, if the Great Tyee chooses to give them to us, would be full redress, and make our hearts glad; and we should henceforth regard the Sitka people as our friends and brothers."

Seward turned to Davis and said, "I think you can afford to give them 36 blankets."

The General was pleased. So were the people of Klukwan and Sitka. They had been unable to travel safely to each other's territory for years, and many had relatives who had married into the other village. The resolution meant families could reunite.

Seward then invited the Chilkats to dine with him on board the *Active*. As evening fell, a flotilla of brightly painted canoes came down the river and the guests swarmed on board. Koh'klux astonished his visitors "by appearing accurately attired in a neat suit of black broadcloth."

The leading men sat in the main cabin with the skylight open. Wives and lower-ranking Indians sat around the deck opening and passed the plates around. The *Active*'s cooks did a pretty good job of creating a feast out of their limited larder.

Among the instruments Davidson had with him was a camera. One regrets that he didn't use it to get a picture of Koh'klux; none seem to exist. A photograph of the giant chief in a suit such as Lincoln would have worn, looming over the diminutive Seward, the co-author of the Emancipation Proclamation standing next to one of the last slave owners in America, both beaming, scarred faces and all, would be an image for the ages.

On the trip back to Sitka Seward made notes for the speech he was to give to the citizens of Sitka. The notes specifically thanked Alaska Natives for his reception. "I appreciate these hospitalities and kindnesses all the more because they have come up to me in the very simple forms ... which only could be expected from a small and mixed community collected together on the outward verge of society."

The transcript of the speech does not include the thanks to indigenous Alaskans or mention a mixed community, but it singles out Koh'klux as "a very intelligent chief."

To the gentlemen of Sitka ("gentle" is crossed out in the notes), Seward predicted that the world would need the resources of the region and that pleasure-seekers would be drawn "by scenery which surpasses in sublimity that of either the Alps, the Apennines, the Alleghenies or the Rocky Mountains."

On August 14 the *Active* departed Sitka. Stops were made in Wrangell, where there had been reports of gold, and Fort Tongass, near modern Ketchikan.

Seward's cabins were full of souvenirs, purchases and gifts. They including a wounded bald eagle, "captured after a sturdy fight."

Twenty-eight: To Mexico

During the voyage south, Seward visited Victoria, Astoria and Portland, traveling up the Columbia River by riverboat as far as the Dalles before returning to San Francisco.

From there the Seward family voyaged to Southern California and then returned north via a stagecoach in what sounds like the greatest adventure of the entire trip. They camped out under the stars alongside settlers arriving by wagon train. They passed a grizzly bear chewing on a carcass, were confronted by vigilantes looking for horse thieves and, while spending the night at a dilapidated mission, had their rooms invaded by a desperado. Anna Seward chased him off.

While in California Seward accepted an invitation from the Mexican government to pay a state visit. Benito Juarez appreciated the fact that Seward had maintained steady diplomatic pressure on France and, in the end, allowed Mexicans to decisively settle the matter themselves without American interference.

But Seward's decision to make the trip drew condemnation from some. "Pray declare war with Mexico," wrote one of the offended. "Disarm that abominable population. I am in hopes to see yet the stars & stripes flying over all God's heathens."

Mexico, however, continued the royal reception that had started in San Francisco and greeted Seward as a national hero. He was feted at banquets and serenaded along his route. He toured historic buildings, factories and schools. Juarez himself escorted the travelers to a fine mansion in the capital and, with a smile, announced, "Mr. Seward, this is your house."

Seward spent three months in Mexico, relishing every minute. When a short part of the trip was taken by train rather than carriage he complained that it was moving too fast to enjoy the scenery.

He was struck by cultural differences. "The word 'Indian' in Mexico is applied to a race widely different from the savages of the

United States. They are civilized and Christian people, neat, intelligent and industrious, kind-hearted and affectionate."

After a sea voyage via Cuba, almost one year after leaving the State Department, Seward finally returned to Auburn. The trip had taken a toll. Difficulty in raising his arms had become more pronounced and friends found him "subdued."

But the trip to Alaska and Mexico had reawakened his lifelong love of travel. He displayed the Tlingit art in his library. He built a spacious enclosure for the eagle and doted on it. The bird seemed to develop a personal relationship with "the wise macaw."

And he immediately made plans for his most ambitious journey, a circumnavigation of the globe.

Twenty-nine: Around the World

Olive Risley Seward, Seward's adopted daughter, who co-authored his account of his trip around the world. From the Library of Congress.

Steam connected the world of 1870. Railroads across Europe, India and the United States meant continents could be crossed in days. Ocean voyages that once took months now lasted weeks. The idea of round-the-world trips for recreation was beginning to stir in the popular imagination. Thomas Cook began arranging such tours in 1872. Jules Verne's "Around the World in 80 Days" was published in 1873.

Seward beat them all. He left Auburn in August of 1870 with his nephew George Seward, a consul assigned to China, and former

Postmaster General Alexander Randall, their wives, an old friend named Hanson Risley and Risley's daughters, Hattie and Olive.

Olive Risley had been Fanny's friend. Since Fanny's death she had grown close to Seward, who saw in her a reflection of his daughter — well-read, intellectual, a young woman who aspired to be a writer and have a meaningful career beyond wife and mother.

It was agreed that Olive would keep notes and help Seward write a book about the trip. With his arms and hands failing him, he needed a secretary. Frederick would not be available this time.

The resulting book, discursive in tone, gives insight into Seward's thinking.

While taking the train through Elko, Nevada, "we find a wretched and squalid remnant of the Shoshones. Must these Indian races indeed perish before the march of the white man? One cannot but hope that the Aztecs of Mexico may prove an exception to the elsewhere universal process of extermination."

Seward declined to meet either Chinese settlers or anti-Chinese groups in San Francisco, but made this point: "The Republican party have lately acquiesced in the policy of exclusion, which has been insisted upon so long and so strenuously by the Democratic party. Mr. Seward protests firmly against this, and teaches that immigration and expansion are the main and inseparable elements of civilization on the American Continent."

The month-long Pacific voyage on the side-wheeler *China* became boring. A route following the Aleutians would give travelers more opportunity for shore excursions, the authors said.

They were enamored with the beauty of Japan. "If we must live in a town, give us one like Nagasaki!"

Olive does not appear to have been present when Seward met the Mikado; signs on the imperial grounds read, "No horses or women."

The imperial robes and elaborate headdress "reminded Mr. Seward of some of the efforts in mythology to represent a deity sitting in the clouds. What the Mikado and his court thought of the costumes of his visitors, with their uncovered heads, square, swallow-tailed dress-coats, tight white cravats, tighter pantaloons, and stiff, black boots, we shall never know. Who shall pronounce between nations in matters of costume?"

The party broke up in Shanghai. The Randalls went home and George was obliged to stay at his duty station in Shanghai. Widower Seward would complete the trek alone in the company of two girls in their 20s.

Such arrangements would raise eyebrows now. In the 1870s they were downright scandalous. So Seward adopted Olive, gave her the family name and, in Beijing, drew up a new will making her his co-heir along with his surviving children by Frances.

His sons, who knew their father better than anyone else, understood. All were successful in their own right, they didn't need his money; there would be no reason to quarrel over the will. Furthermore, he needed help to continue the journey. Randall had told them he could no longer use his hands for most purposes.

Like good children everywhere, they wanted their parent to be happy. They knew he loved Olive and that she was devoted to him. They were pleased to think that this trip of a lifetime was bringing him joy. If Olive could make his dream come true, then they could cheerfully embrace her as a sister.

Hanson Risley, who had left the group in San Francisco, was not happy about it. He wrote demanding that Seward return his daughters. Seward ignored him.

From China the route went through Southeast Asia, Saigon, Singapore, Java, across India and the Arabian Sea to Suez. Seward spent May in Egypt, where he marveled at the Pyramids. He went on to Constantinople and speculated that the Turkish Empire would soon collapse due to sectarian differences and a lack of industry. By contrast, Eastern Europe was booming. He compared the factories and modern transportation infrastructure favorably with the eastern United States.

The group saw Athens, Budapest, Vienna, Italy, Geneva and Berlin. They made a swing through Paris, which Seward found in "sad condition," the population "universally discouraged." The Franco-Prussian War had just ended with the abdication of Napoleon III followed by the bloody suppression of an insurrection in Paris that left thousands dead and major buildings burned.

After a stop in London, Seward returned to Auburn in October of 1871. His first words were, "How's the bird?" — the eagle he'd brought back from Alaska. Its cage was the first place he went to when he arrived at his house.

William Jr. was now the proprietor of the Auburn home, but William Sr. still took his place at the head of the table. He could no longer cut his own food or pick up a deck of cards. He made a carriage ride daily, and even rowed, an exercise that did not require raising his arms above chest level. He also experienced greater pain in his face and neck, probably from the wounds of the assassination attempt. His stride, which had long remained robust, became a shuffle. Ramps were installed to let him move around the house.

A succession of visitors came to see him, old political friends, old enemies and celebrities like Ole Bull, the famed Norwegian violinist. In early 1872 he played for Seward at the Auburn mansion and told **The New York Times** that "he found the veteran statesman in remarkably good health, and engaged with great ardor in preparing for the press reminiscences of his recent grand journey round the globe."

Olive became a fixture at the Seward House, writing the travel book with Seward, a full-time job for both of them. But his breath became shorter each day.

On October 10, 1872, he dressed as usual and began working on the book with Olive. He grew tired, lay down on a green couch in the study and "was attacked by a difficulty of breathing."

A doctor came and advised the family that the end was near. Seward heard the remark and "received it with a placid smile, as if neither unexpected nor unwelcome."

William Jr., his wife, Jenny, and Olive were with him. Jenny leaned close and asked, "Father, have you anything to say to us?"

He opened his eyes one last time. "Nothing," he said. "Love one another."

He died around 4 p.m.

Epilogue

Jefferson Columbus Davis left Alaska in 1870. In 1873 he ended the long-running Modoc War in Northern California and Southern Oregon. The hanging of Modoc leader Kintpuash, or "Captain Jack," in October of that year was the formal end of the California Genocide, although practices like sterilizing Indian women continued into the 1970s.

"William H. Seward's Travels Around the World" was a best-seller. The royalties made Olive Risley Seward rich. She founded the Literary Society of Washington, D.C. and died in that city in 1908. She never married.

Koh'klux became known as a peacemaker, defusing hostilities, sometimes using blankets or money in cases requiring restitution. He was among the chiefs who assigned land for a mission school in a place that later became the city of Haines and the site of the site of a U.S. military base from the Gold Rush through World War II, Fort William Seward.

Twenty years after the Emancipation Proclamation, Koh'klux freed his own slaves out of respect, it was said, for "The Great Tyee."

The Presbyterian missionaries did not like him. He remained, one wrote, "a heathen of heathens." But they were nonetheless in awe of him. The aging chief greeted whites wearing a magnificent cloak made from hundreds of chinchillas. It would have been the envy of fashion aficionados in New York. Near the top was a label with the words, "To Chief Shathich, from his friend, Wm. H. Seward."

He died in 1889. The next generation of Tlingits produced politicians and lawyers. After decades of litigation and legislation Alaska Native land claims were recognized by the federal government in 1971.

Alaska's economic importance became clear after Seward's death, when major gold discoveries were made in Juneau and on the Kenai

Peninsula, followed by the Klondike Gold Rush and subsequent bonanzas in Nome and Fairbanks.

Its strategic importance became clear in World War II, when warplanes were sent to Russia over the Bering Strait and Japanese and American soldiers died in the Aleutian Islands fighting the only land battle between armies in North America since the Civil War. In the Cold War it became — and continues to be — America's first line of defense against nuclear attack.

Alaska gained statehood in 1959, the fulfillment of what many scholars and most Alaskans say was Seward's greatest achievement.

One may wonder what would have happened had the gun of Lewis Powell, Seward's assigned assassin, had worked and John Wilkes Booth's gun had misfired, instead of the other way around. If Seward had been killed and Lincoln survived.

A familiar line of thinking goes that the reintegration of the South and North might have gone more smoothly. Lincoln would still have needed to deal with the radicals, but he was a far more able politician than Johnson and, even without Seward's advice, could have convinced Congress to follow his agenda. The postwar period would have been better for both blacks and whites in the South and in the country at large.

But the map of the country would not include Alaska. The 49th state is American almost entirely because of Seward's diligence in the negotiations and his quick reflexes when the Tsar finally tendered an offer. Other able statesmen might have been able to do it. Or maybe not.

If not, then perhaps the Russian flag would still fly over New Archangel and Kodiak. Or, more likely, Alaska would be part of Canada.

Many of Seward's aspirations eventually became reality. Hawaii, the Virgin Islands and Puerto Rico are U.S. possessions. World commerce travels through the Panama Canal and along the Great Circle route through the Aleutian Islands. At this writing a high-speed communications cable is being laid that connects Alaska with Europe and Asia via the Arctic Ocean and Bering Sea, a modern incarnation of the Bering Strait telegraph plan.

But Seward's real "greatest achievement" is the continued existence of the United States of America. His actions during the Secession Winter of 1861, the *Trent* Affair and the Johnson impeachment arguably saved the country, or at least gave it the shape and scope we recognize today.

The man who bought Alaska is buried at Fort Hill Cemetery in Auburn, not far from where Harriet Tubman rests. His wife and Cornelia on his left side, Fanny and his sons on his right. All are covered by similar sarcophagi. Seward's tomb is decorated with an urn that bears the three words he most wanted to be remembered by.

"He was faithful."

Bibliography

Black, Lydia T. *Russians in Alaska, 1732-1867*. Fairbanks: University of Alaska Press, 2004

Chevigny, Hector *Russian America: The Great Alaskan Venture, 1741-1867*. New York: Viking Press, 1965

Christensen, Annie Constance *Letters from the Governor's Wife: A View of Russian Alaska 1859-1862*. Aarhus, Denmark: Aarhus University Press, 2005

Dauenhauer, Nora Marks, Dauenhauer, Richard and Black, Lydia T. (eds.) *Anóoshi Lingít Aaní Ká / Russians in Tlingit America: The Battles of Sitka, 1802 and 1804*. Seattle: University of Washington Press, 2008

Emmons, George Thornton and De Laguna, Frederica *The Tlingit Indians*. Seattle: University of Washington Press, 1991

Goodwin, Doris Kearns *Team of Rivals: The Political Genius of Abraham Lincoln*. New York: Simon & Schuster, 2005

Hughes, Nathaniel Cheairs, Jr. and Whitney, Gordon D. *Jefferson Davis in Blue: The Life of Sherman's Relentless Warrior*. Baton Rouge: Lousiana State University Press, 2002

Naske, Claus-M. and Slotnick, Herman E. *Alaska: A History*. Norman: University of Oklahoma Press, 2014

Madley, Benjamin *An American Genocide: The United States and the California Indian Catastrophe*. New Haven: Yale University Press, 2016

Seward, Frederick *William Seward at Washington as Senator and Secretary of State: A Memoire of His Life, with Selections from His Letters, 1861- 1872*. New York: Derby and Miller, 1891

Seward, Olive Risley (with Seward, William H.) *William H. Seward's Travels Around the World*. New York: D. Appleton and Company, 1873

Seward, William Henry *Autobiography of William H. Seward, from 1801 to 1834*. New York, D. Appleton and Company, 1877

Sipes, Ernest *Into the Savage Land: The Alas... urnal of Edward Adams*. Surrey, British Columbia: Hancock ... se, 2007

Stahr, Walter *Seward: Lincoln's Indispensable Man*. New York: Simon & Schuster, 2012

Van Deusen, Glyndon G. *William Henry Seward*. Oxford: Oxford University Press, 1967

About the Author

Photo by Erik Hill.

A native of Pampa, Texas, Michael Dunham lived as a small child in the western Alaska Native village of Quinhagak in the 1950s where he saw elders said to have been born when the territory was part of the Russian Empire. He is a graduate of Anchorage West High School.

After Alaska became a state, he studied history at the University of Washington in Seattle. He graduated Summa Cum Laude from the University of St. Thomas in Houston, Texas. Over the past 50 years he has worked in a variety of jobs at Alaska radio stations and as an editor, reporter and arts critic at the ***Anchorage Times***, ***Anchorage Daily News*** and ***Alaska Dispatch News***.

Dunham is the author of several entries in ***"Frommer's Guide to Alaska"*** and has been a contributor to the BBC, ***Opera***, ***Orion*** and ***Reason*** magazines. He is the co-editor of Osahito Miyaoka's ***"A Grammar of Central Yupik."*** Contact him at Box 220152, Anchorage, AK 99522.